TABLE OF CONTENTS

INTRODUCTION

Gen 18:17-19

"The LORD said, 'Shall I hide from Abraham what I am about to do, since Abraham will surely become a great and mighty nation, and in him all the nations of the earth will be blessed? For I have chosen him, so that he may command his children and his household after him to keep the way of the LORD by doing righteousness and justice, so that the LORD may bring upon Abraham what He has spoken about him.'"

God will not hide His secret plans if He can find those who understand trans-generational ministry. We must be able to bring those under our oversight into the obedience of the faith through the grace and apostleship He has given us. Abraham commanded his children and his household after him to keep the way of the Lord by doing righteousness and justice.

God is trans-generational in His plans and purposes. He does not want to keep raising one man every few years who only serves his time on earth without leaving a legacy in the things which God has richly deposited into his life for others to continue in. What God is giving to a man is not just for himself and for his lifetime, but for his generation and for the generations to come.

Lam 5:19

"You, O LORD, rule forever; Your throne is from generation to generation."

Dan 4:3

""How great are His signs And how mighty are His wonders! His kingdom is an everlasting kingdom And His dominion is from generation to generation."

Is 51:8

"'For the moth will eat them like a garment, And the grub will eat them like wool. But My righteousness will be forever, And My salvation to all generations.'"

Ps 33:11

"The counsel of the LORD stands forever, The plans of His heart from generation to generation."

His throne, His dominion, His salvation and all His plans are for all generations! Even though one generation passes and another comes into existence, His mercy and lovingkindness leaves an indelible mark on each one of them. Though a curse may last till the third and fourth generation, but the mercy of God lasts a thousand generation *(Ex 20:5-6)*.

Thus, God is looking for the continuity of legacy and of His purposes here on earth. God will reveal His secret plans to those who will make every effort to raise the next generation and the ensuing ones to walk in that which He has begun with them. He will reveal strategies for national transformation. He will release His miracle power for those who are ready to impart it into others, empowering them to continue what God has begun in their midst.

2 Tim 1:3-4

"I thank God, whom I serve with a clear conscience the way my forefathers did, as I constantly remember you in my prayers night and day, longing to see you, even as I recall your tears, so that I may be filled with joy."

The apostle Paul, who has served God with a clear conscience like his forefathers now instructs Timothy, the third generation, to continue the legacy placed into him. In fact, he reminds Timothy that his grandmother and mother have also provided a strong contribution to that which he is carrying within him. Paul exhorts him to stir up and rekindle what has been placed and imparted into him so that God can crown it with the spirit of power, of love and of a sound mind.

2 Tim 1:6-7
"For this reason I remind you to kindle afresh the gift of God which is in you through the laying on of my hands. For God has not given us a spirit of timidity, but of power and love and discipline."

These generations were meant to become connected together to fulfill the same destiny and complete the same purpose. This spirit of intimidation was preventing Timothy from rising to the occasion. Paul's exhortation was for Timothy to wage an accurate warfare against these distractions and intimidations so that both the generations, Paul and Timothy, can continue to move forward in the legacy of the forefathers. He needed not be ashamed, but could join Paul for the furtherance of the Kingdom.

2 Tim 1:8
"Therefore do not be ashamed of the testimony of our Lord or of me His prisoner, but join with me in suffering for the gospel according to the power of God,"

When Timothy had found his footing, he was instructed both to retain the standard of sound words which he had received, and to guard the "treasure" which has been entrusted to him.

2 Tim 1:13-14
"Retain the standard of sound words which you have heard from me, in the faith and love which are in Christ Jesus. Guard, through the Holy Spirit who dwells in us, the treasure which has been entrusted to you."

Paul further exhorts Timothy to look for faithful men who will also be able to teach others the pattern he had placed into Timothy.

2 Tim 2:2
"The things which you have heard from me in the presence of many witnesses, entrust these to faithful men who will be able to teach others also."

This would be the fourth generation. This pattern of reproducing men is clearly seen in Paul's apostolic ministry. He gathers the disciples of Apollos, upgrading and updating them into the current move of God. Though Apollos was fervent in the old and mighty in the Scriptures, he was only acquainted with the baptism of John. The tragic reality of the present day religious institutions that are producing experts in the outdated teachings, cannot be denied. They are leaving behind thousands of believers who are "lost in transition". Many of these Christian leaders need to be taken aside and re-schooled in the Spirit. They need to be taught *"more accurately the way of God" (Acts 18:24-26).* Their disciples also need to be updated and upgraded with present truth so that they can progressively make the transition into the new from the old order of things that are currently becoming obsolete!

The present apostolic move is bringing clear accurate doctrines so that believers who have been disciples of the present day "Apollos" can move forward without losing out on their inheritance. Thus, a whole generation is being discipled by the current apostolic move. God is saving them from being plundered by false doctrines and cleverly devised tales *(2 Pet 1:16).* When revelation knowledge is cut off from our lives, the next generation will be cut off from their own inheritance.

> Hos 4:6
> *"My people are destroyed for lack of knowledge. Because you have rejected knowledge, I also will reject you from being My priest. Since you have forgotten the law of your God, I also will forget your children."*

There is a powerful believers movement that is about to break out in these concluding years of destiny. God is raising a generation of fathers to bring to maturity a whole generation of sons who have been orphaned along the way. This generation is sitting outside the walls of Jericho and of their inheritance. God wants the current leadership to bring them into their inheritance by the process of fathering them to become the true sons of God here on the earth. This generation will cross over and possess the land. This generation will come into the covenant by coming through the process of the circumcision of their hearts and the renewing of the minds. This generation will have power to bring the fulfillment of all the words that has been spoken to their forefathers. They will come into the reality of all that have been promised and prophesied.

This finishing generation will be crowned with a generous company of fathers around them from whom they will draw and receive impartation. Like Moses to Joshua, like Samuel to David and like Paul to Timothy, this generation will have true apostolic fathers who will nurture and empower them to come into the fulfillment of the purposes and promises of the forefathers.

This book is the book of hope for those who are looking for the finishing generation. This book will inspire you to become the generation that matters. It will reveal to you the state of the true believers who are emerging in the true church of our Lord Jesus Christ. You would love to be in Church, because His church will be filled with this new breed of breakthrough believers. Pastors will love to attend the church they have been pastoring, as those "sons in the house" will become their crown and joy. God's words declare that He will act by His own arm and bring this about in our days.

> Is 59:21
> *"'As for Me, this is My covenant with them,' says the LORD: 'My Spirit which is upon you, and My words which I have put in your mouth shall not depart from your mouth, nor from the mouth of your offspring, nor from the mouth of your offspring's offspring,' says the LORD, 'from now and forever.'"*

> Is 60:21-22
> *"'Then all your people will be righteous; They will possess the land forever, The branch of My planting, The work of My hands, That I may be glorified. The smallest one will become a clan, And the least one a mighty nation. I, the LORD, will hasten it in its time.'"*

Chapter One

A Prophetic Generation

There is a generation rising on the earth today that is causing the cloud of witnesses in the heavens to rejoice. It is in their manifestation, as the sons of God here on the earth, that will cause everything around them to become redefined. All of the prophetic dimensions in the spirit realm have been highly activated. God is commanding and sending His angels and messengers to bring His royal assignment to these pursued ones. The fulfillment of prophecies and prophetic purposes will be activated because of this generation rising across the earth.

The prophetic fulfillment of many of God's promises will earth itself in this generation. God will rise upon them and manifest His awesome power to reveal Himself in the earth. All the activities surrounding the life of Jesus were aligned to the prophetic purposes of God. It happened in His life so that Scripture concerning Him can be fulfilled.

> Matt 2:15
> *"He remained there until the death of Herod. This was to fulfill what had been spoken by the Lord through the prophet: 'OUT OF EGYPT I CALLED MY SON.'"*

Matt 1:22
"Now all this took place to fulfill what was spoken by the Lord through the prophet:"

Matt 2:17
"Then what had been spoken through Jeremiah the prophet was fulfilled:"

Matt 4:14
"This was to fulfill what was spoken through Isaiah the prophet:"

God is now preparing a generation that will "walk the talk" and walk into the fulfillment of what was spoken by God concerning them.

Ps 102:18
"This will be written for the generation to come, That a people yet to be created may praise the LORD."

Whatever that is written about them becomes the foundational base for the character formation and development of these breakthrough believers. God is causing the fulfillment of His words to precipitate upon this unique generation.

The prophecies of *Isaiah* that a virgin will bear a child was floating over hundreds of years. It could not become fulfilled until God has found a vessel worthy and sanctified for this very purpose. She found favor in the sight of God and declared boldly for God to execute His Word in total fulfillment in her life.

Luke 1:38
"And Mary said, 'Behold, the bondslave of the Lord; may it be done to me according to your word.' And the angel departed from her."

The word of God was fulfilled in her and the Holy Spirit overshadowed her. She did not just want to hear the word, but desired that God will do according to the word.

This generation of Jesus will bring God's word into reality. All that God has been saying to us about our destiny and assignment here on earth can come into immediate operation if we become yielded to the processes of God's dealing on our lives.

God is raising that significant company of believers across the earth who will not abort their prophetic journey, because the word of God is pulsating in their hearts. They possess the dreams of God in their hearts. The Word of the Spirit is impregnated in their hearts. The core of their bones are laden with the prophecies of the future. Like Joseph, they have been "taken" by God for a future time of manifestation.

The freedom and liberty the Holy Spirit will have among us will be significant because of this new generation that is rising. The old generation who will not mix the word of God with faith *(Heb 4:2)*, will be cut off from their future inheritance. This Finishing Generation will have the faith to believe the word and will desire its accurate fulfillment over their lives.

> Heb 3:12, 19
> *"Take care, brethren, that there not be in any one of you an evil, unbelieving heart that falls away from the living God. ... So we see that they were not able to enter because of unbelief."*

> Heb 4:11
> *"Therefore let us be diligent to enter that rest, so that no one will fall, through following the same example of disobedience."*

A vision I had early in the year 2000, has become an inspiration for many pastors across the earth. I saw a huge brick factory with all kinds of bricks being made. Ordinary, colored, glazed, designed and other varieties of bricks were being made in this factory. Then after a period of time, I saw hundreds of large trucks carrying these bricks (varieties of them) to different places and distributing them to the many construction sites across the country. The builders were waiting for the arrival of these bricks to complete their assignments and projects.

God revealed to me that many churches are only functioning as brick factories.

They have made the bricks, and have maintained and housed them in the warehouses. The believers are not participating in anything that will bring them to peak performance in their potential, nor are they moving closer towards God's destiny for their lives. They are forced to maintain the status quo of their environment. I hear God say that the greatest exodus is about to happen. It is not an exodus out of Egypt or Babylon, but an exodus out of religion and religious institutions.

God will move these living bricks He has redeemed and fashioned, toward the builders He has raised and assigned to build His House. These builders are apostolic pastors who have received the mandate and the blueprints to build accurately a House that cannot be shaken or taken!

God is redistributing these living bricks, and they will each find their own companions and family who have the same characteristics. God will bring Judah back to his people!

> Deut 33:7
> *"And this regarding Judah; so he said, 'Hear, O LORD, the voice of Judah, And bring him to his people. With his hands he contended for them, And may You be a help against his adversaries.'"*

Those who are building accurately according to the apostolic blueprints will see an influx of people and a supernatural harvest.

I was in the spirit during one of our Celebration Sundays, when I heard demonic voices mocking saying, "See you could have filled this auditorium with hundreds more if you had compromised just a little!" Then I heard the voice of the Lord saying "Now you only have those who are precious!" Let us allow God to help us gather only the precious and not the trash!

So many pastors and leaders have been enticed to build big and build quick. They epitomize the parable of the mustard seed which grows larger than the garden plant it should be, and becomes a large tree where the birds of the air come and nest in their branches. When we force growth and choose abnormal growth, we run the risk of having the flesh, and ultimately, demonic spirits

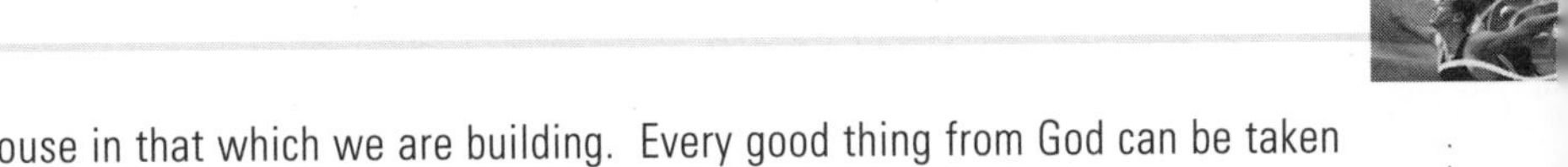

house in that which we are building. Every good thing from God can be taken over by the fleshly lust of men, and become perverted to fulfill the kingdom of self that rules them *(Is 59:13-14)*.

Those who have been holding on to the truth and the convictions of the Holy Spirit, will not loose out on the best that God has for us. Those who have become a prey to the enemy because they have chosen not to compromise with kingdom values of honor, integrity and accountability, will be justly rewarded. Our toils and our tears which we have sowed will be replaced by the harvest of this new generation, born of the spirit.

God is releasing these bricks that are already cut, fashioned and designed and they are coming towards the houses that have been accurately aligned to apostolic patterns.

God has seen the injustice done to so many of His servants in the building of His Church. He has seen that there are "wicked men among His people" *(Jer 5:26)* and because of them the righteous are oppressed in the Kingdom.

> Is 59:15-16
> *"Yes, truth is lacking; And he who turns aside from evil makes himself a prey. Now the LORD saw, And it was displeasing in His sight that there was no justice. And He saw that there was no man, And was astonished that there was no one to intercede; Then His own arm brought salvation to Him, And His righteousness upheld Him."*

God is acting on His own accord and He will bring deliverance for the righteous. Truth will no longer stumble in the streets. Righteousness will not stand far away and not deliver. We will not be hoping for light and find darkness. Our day of deliverance is here, as God will move sovereignly among His people. The heavens are pulsating with prophetic fulfillment. His Word and His Spirit are being sent to invade the hearts of the righteous. The condition in the temple and its priesthood are about to see drastic changes. We welcome the apostolic invasion of God into His Church. It is His sovereign coming into the temple that will cause the new generation to be revealed.

Matt 21:15-16
"But when the chief priests and the scribes saw the wonderful things that He had done, and the children who were shouting in the temple, 'Hosanna to the Son of David,' they became indignant and said to Him, 'Do You hear what these children are saying?' And Jesus said to them, 'Yes; have you never read, "OUT OF THE MOUTH OF INFANTS AND NURSING BABIES YOU HAVE PREPARED PRAISE FOR YOURSELF"?'"

It is His coming into His Church that will cleanse the leadership, and bring about acceptance and wholeness among the people.

Mal 3:3-4
"He will sit as a smelter and purifier of silver, and He will purify the sons of Levi and refine them like gold and silver, so that they may present to the LORD offerings in righteousness. Then the offering of Judah and Jerusalem will be pleasing to the LORD as in the days of old and as in former years."

His coming manifested presence will cause the church to see national revival and reformation in the society. He will act swiftly in the society.

Mal 3:5
"'Then I will draw near to you for judgment; and I will be a swift witness against the sorcerers and against the adulterers and against those who swear falsely, and against those who oppress the wage earner in his wages, the widow and the orphan, and those who turn aside the alien and do not fear Me,' says the LORD of hosts."

Mal 4:5-6
"'Behold, I am going to send you Elijah the prophet before the coming of the great and terrible day of the LORD. He will restore the hearts of the fathers to their children and the hearts of the children to their fathers, so that I will not come and smite the land with a curse.'"

We welcome this new generation that God is raising and releasing on the earth. They carry the hope of the future generations, and the dreams of the past generations. Like Joseph, their rising will bring release and protection to many.

Be blessed by the rising of this Finishing Generation. Partner with this company of breakthrough believers to finish destiny together as we bring down the curtains of time on the age of iniquity!

Chapter Two

FASHIONED BY GOD TO FULFILL DESTINY

The Lord gave me a prophetic vision that changed the view of how I saw the future of His church. I saw the hand of the Lord plucked into the earth and brought forth into His hand an unborn fetus. He clasped His fingers together and His hand became like a womb containing the baby. The baby started to grow strong and into full maturity receiving life and all the nutrients from His hands. At full term, the Lord released the clasp of His hand and set the baby on the earth. The baby stood up and as he started to walk he became a man. Wherever he went, more men like him were coming out into the streets and the highways were filled with ones like him. Then I heard the voice of the Lord declaring, "I am fashioning a new generation on the earth by My own hands. They will not be the product of the environment, or of human endeavor. They will be born of My Spirit and will know My ways. It is this generation which I have fashioned by My hands that I will entrust My final assignment to. I will trust them because My hands have fashioned them. I will entrust them with all My power to bring what I began to a completion. You will be there for them to father them and lead them across into their inheritance ..."

I am already seeing a new generation on the earth, and I know their presence will become clearer to us in the days ahead. This generation is now being

fashioned by His hands. He is making them the vessels He wants them to be so that they will be empowered to fulfill their assignment on the earth.

Ps 102:12-17

"But You, O LORD, abide forever, And Your name to all generations. You will arise and have compassion on Zion; For it is time to be gracious to her, For the appointed time has come. Surely Your servants find pleasure in her stones And feel pity for her dust. So the nations will fear the name of the LORD And all the kings of the earth Your glory. For the LORD has built up Zion; He has appeared in His glory. He has regarded the prayer of the destitute And has not despised their prayer."

Ps 102:18-22

"This will be written for the generation to come, That a people yet to be created may praise the LORD. For He looked down from His holy height; From heaven the LORD gazed upon the earth, To hear the groaning of the prisoner, To set free those who were doomed to death, That men may tell of the name of the LORD in Zion And His praise in Jerusalem, When the peoples are gathered together, And the kingdoms, to serve the LORD."

There are some distinctive features of this finishing generation of breakthrough believers. These features will help us identify them in our midst, as they are the planting of the Lord in whom He will be glorified.

They Have Stature To Represent God

The first feature this generation will reveal is that they have grown in stature to fully represent God. They are no longer a desolate nation or a destitute people, nor are their prayers despised. They are finding their place of favor before God. He is responding to them in compassion, and listening to the voice of their prayers *(v. 13, 17)*. They are drawing the attention of God, even through the slightest groaning of their soul. He is looking down from His holy height to show Himself strong on their behalf *(v. 19)*. Even those sent by the Lord to her, are delighted by what they see among her. The living stones are manifesting God's favor and are radiant in His glory *(v. 14)*. The Lord has built up Zion and He is appearing in that which He, Himself has built. The glory of God is crowing what He has built and approved *(v. 16)*. Can you see beyond the regular Church and the physical gathering of men? Can you see that the favor of God is upon us to take us to Zion? God will stretch out His hands from Zion and rule in the midst of His enemies *(Ps 110:2)*. The church comes into this measure of favor when she comes into the maturity of Zion. She will bring the re-definition on the earth. Nations will fear the name of the Lord and the kings will come to her rising brightness *(Is 60:3)*.

Stature is the position of favor obtained in God as we yield to the dealings of God in our lives until He finds us a trustworthy steward who will represent Him fully, and be bestowed with the necessary grace, provision and wisdom to finish Kingdom purposes here on the earth. It is an extraordinary state of maturity that positions us to represent Him fully.

> 1 Kings 17:1
> *"Now Elijah the Tishbite, who was of the settlers of Gilead, said to Ahab, "As the LORD, the God of Israel lives, before whom I stand, surely there shall be neither dew nor rain these years, except by my word.""*

Stature is different from status as it is only obtained by God's approval and attested to us by God's supernatural provision and grace. Status, on the other hand, can be easily given by men to men.

Elijah found the favor of God's presence. He leared to dwell in the secret place of the Most High. He learned to operate from that new address. He was standing where God is standing and he was operating on God's behalf, fully representing Him. The word of the Lord in his mouth was as powerful as the word of the Lord in God's mouth. The elements of the earth responded to him as they would do to God, the Creator.

1 Kings 16:34

"In his days Hiel the Bethelite built Jericho; he laid its foundations with the loss of Abiram his firstborn, and set up its gates with the loss of his youngest son Segub, according to the word of the LORD, which He spoke by Joshua the son of Nun."

Joshua also knew such statute before God, in that his oath taken over Jericho was honored in full measure by God. Interestingly, it was what Joshua spoke that became as it were the oracles of God.

Joshua 10:14

"There was no day like that before it or after it, when the LORD listened to the voice of a man; for the LORD fought for Israel."

They Have Power to Execute His Word

This finishing generation is made to bring the word of God into fulfillment. Everything that has been spoken about them will be fulfilled in them. They are the prophetic company prophets have prophesied about. They are the exact representation of what has been spoken. They are the living epistles of Christ, not written with ink, but with the spirit of the living God. Not on tablets of stone, but on tablets of human hearts *(2 Cor 3:3)*. This generation will be the living proof of the reality of the proceeding word that has gone forth. They will walk the talk. They will be the demonstration of what had been spoken. They will walk prophecies into fulfillment. They will bring the promises of God into reality, and the commandments of God into execution.

Ps 102:18

"This will be written for the generation to come, That a people yet to be created may praise the LORD."

What is written and what has been spoken is finding fulfillment in this unique company. When we carry that proceeding word inside our hearts and fulfill

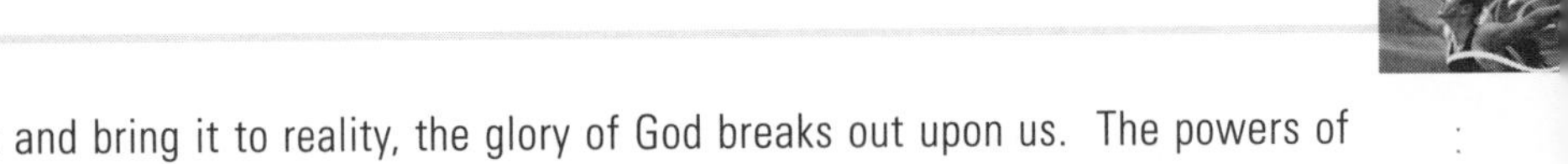

it and bring it to reality, the glory of God breaks out upon us. The powers of darkness are moved out of our territory. We display what was invisible, into the visible realm so that others can see. This will allow others to have access into the supernatural and all that God has desired for man to have and become.

> Jn 1:14
> *"And the Word became flesh, and dwelt among us, and we saw His glory, glory as of the only begotten from the Father, full of grace and truth."*

Those who watch our lives can find a pattern and an access code to enter into what was invisible in the heavenly realm. What was invisible and what was impossible have been brought out into the possibility realm and have been made to become a reality in their lives.

> Luke 1:37-38
> *"'For nothing will be impossible with God.' And Mary said, 'Behold, the bondslave of the Lord; may it be done to me according to your word.' And the angel departed from her."*

The prophecies of Isaiah concerning "a virgin shall bear a child" was floating in the spiritual realm for hundreds of years, wanting to earth itself into a generation that will see its reality. The angel Gabriel was sent with that specific word to meet Mary. The ordinary woman became the favored one of God. The insignificant one become the blessed among woman.

She requested that what was spoken to her, must now be done to her! She knew that the word of God spoken to her cannot be fulfilled in the natural way. She needed God to do whatever it takes to make it a reality in her life. She was ready for God to work upon her until this word became fulfilled.

> Rom 4:19-21
> *"Without becoming weak in faith he contemplated his own body, now as good as dead since he was about a hundred years old, and the deadness of Sarah's womb; yet, with respect to the promise of God, he did not waver in unbelief but grew strong in faith,*

giving glory to God, and being fully assured that what God had promised, He was able also to perform."

God who speaks to us is also the God who is able to perform. This finishing generation is able to grow strong in faith without wavering with respect to their faith, being fully assured that God who has promised is well able to perform.

Joseph knew that God's promise to him would become a reality. It was only a matter of time. He lived in anticipation of its fulfillment. He was "taken up" by the thoughts of the prophecies. He was caught up with the excitement of its reality. He was the dreamer. He was living in another world where the words of the dream had already become a reality.

Bartimaeus was blind, but he could see while sitting on the road from Jericho to Jerusalem and he would listed to all the testimonies of how people were healed and delivered by Jesus. He would imagine these events and see them in his mind. Every now and then a smile would rise on his face. The people passing by would ask him why, and he would reply, "I am seeing something." Bartimaeus discovered a whole world out there in his mind. He would escape his physical limitation and enter into the realm of his mind. His mind seemed to have no boundaries or limitations. He saw himself walking freely, totally healed. He saw that day when he would be free to follow Jesus everywhere. He was living in that world of possibilities. Then, one day he heard it was Jesus, the Nazarene, that was passing by his way. His dream fulfiller was knocking on his door.

There is a whole new generation that has discovered the process of how to mix the word with faith and bring it into reality. They are careful in what they listen to as that will form the nature of their lives.

Mark 4:24
"And He was saying to them, 'Take care what you listen to. By your standard of measure it will be measured to you; and more will be given you besides.'"

They are careful in how they listen as it will determine how deep it will go into their hearts.

Luke 8:18
"'So take care how you listen; for whoever has, to him more shall be given; and whoever does not have, even what he thinks he has shall be taken away from him.'"

They are also careful to who they listen to as this will determine the direction in their lives.

Gen 3:11
"And He said, 'Who told you that you were naked? Have you eaten from the tree of which I commanded you not to eat?'"

The "who" that tells us, can determine our course into the future. Jesus warned that we must be sure who is the one who leads us in the last days. This will determine where we would finally arrive!

This prophetic generation will have power to prevail and bring the words written concerning them into a reality.

They Are Prepared For The Future

This finishing generation is being prepared for the future. God is the only One who knows what the future holds. He knows the situations and circumstances that will be there in the future. He will be the One who will fashion this future company with the right ingredients to be the prevailing force in the future.

When the country is constantly under the threat of a future earthquake or volcanic terrors, the building code will carry extra precautionary measure for the construction of the houses in that environment. The future determines what type of elements are needed for the house. Its structures, its foundation and its materials are all determined by what we anticipate could possibly happen in the future.

1 Tim 4:1-3

"But the Spirit explicitly says that in later times some will fall away from the faith, paying attention to deceitful spirits and doctrines of demons, by means of the hypocrisy of liars seared in their own conscience as with a branding iron, men who forbid marriage and advocate abstaining from foods which God has created to be gratefully shared in by those who believe and know the truth."

2 Tim 3:1-5

"But realize this, that in the last days difficult times will come. For men will be lovers of self, lovers of money, boastful, arrogant, revilers, disobedient to parents, ungrateful, unholy, unloving, irreconcilable, malicious gossips, without self-control, brutal, haters of good, treacherous, reckless, conceited, lovers of pleasure rather than lovers of God, holding to a form of godliness, although they have denied its power; Avoid such men as these."

God will fashion this generation with intense care, as they will be brutally tested against the worst environment possible. The evil gates of hell will come crashing against this generation. The Lord will make them out of the finest material that will stand the test of time. They will be living stones. They will be precious stones tested and tried by the fire of God.

1 Pet 2:4-5

"And coming to Him as to a living stone which has been rejected by men, but is choice and precious in the sight of God, you also, as living stones, are being built up as a spiritual house for a holy priesthood, to offer up spiritual sacrifices acceptable to God through Jesus Christ."

There will be something "regal" about this generation as they are a kingdom of priests; a royal priesthood!

They are also kept for the final leg of the race. They are appointed for the release in the future. God will not allow them to become encumbered with the civilian pursuits of today. Their time has not yet come. Others may be released today and

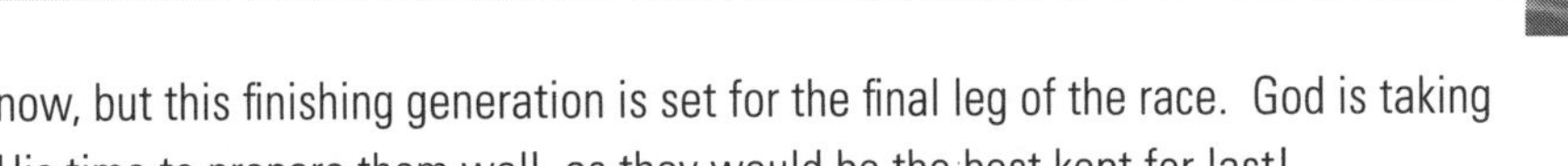

now, but this finishing generation is set for the final leg of the race. God is taking His time to prepare them well, as they would be the best kept for last!

We have not seen a generation like this before. These men and women of the Spirit will cause the minds of men to marvel by their future manifestation as they display the wisdom and maturity of the Son of God in their lives. This generation is hidden in the hollow of His hand. They are in the womb of the dawn, being prepared in God.

> Ps 110:3
> *"Your people will volunteer freely in the day of Your power; In holy array, from the womb of the dawn, Your youth are to You as the dew."*

They will be released at the beginning of the new day before the rising of the dawn!

Like Jacob, this generation will be a product of God's invasion into their lives. Jacob prevailed with God and became a transformed into Israel, a prince with God.

> Gen 32:26
> *"Then he said, 'Let me go, for the dawn is breaking.' But he said, 'I will not let you go unless you bless me.'"*

A new day is dawning. We will not be facing a new day without having prevailed in the God encounter available for us. Our names and nature must be changed so that we can be sufficient to face tomorrow and all it will bring.

They Are Free From The Past

> Ps 102:19-20
> *"For He looked down from His holy height; From heaven the LORD gazed upon the earth, To hear the groaning of the prisoner, To set free those who were doomed to death,"*

There will be supernatural grace on this generation to know God's power to be free in all their deeds. The Son of God will set them free from every hold of satan, sickness and sins. God will hear their groanings and the power of their prayer.

Col 2:14-15
"having canceled out the certificate of debt consisting of decrees against us, which was hostile to us; and He has taken it out of the way, having nailed it to the cross. When He had disarmed the rulers and authorities, He made a public display of them, having triumphed over them through Him."

Every certificate of debt consisting of decrees against them will be removed and cancelled. The sentence of death and the appointment with death will be cancelled on this generation. Those who are doomed to die will be set free from the powers of hell. God is rising on their behalf to scatter all His enemies.

God is showing this generation the process of how to enter into this realm of the Spirit.

Rom 8:10
"If Christ is in you, though the body is dead because of sin, yet the spirit is alive because of righteousness."

When we are born again, the Spirit of Christ dwells in us. We have been recreated into the image and likeness of Jesus Christ. Our spirit has taken on this image of Jesus Christ and we have the full potential of living, acting and becoming like him. Though our spirit is alive, our human body has already tasted sin and death in our soul and in our body. Sin habits are still within our soul and body. Our physical body is moving each day closer to the grave because the wages of sin is death.

Rom 6:23
"For the wages of sin is death, but the free gift of God is eternal life in Christ Jesus our Lord."

So we realize, our spirit is renewed everyday because it is alive and righteous towards God. However, our body struggles to keep pace with the development in our spirit.

> 2 Co 4:16
> *"Therefore we do not lose heart, but though our outer man is decaying, yet our inner man is being renewed day by day."*

We thank God that we do not have to live in this disparity between the spirit development and the state of our physical body that is declining and moving towards the grave.

> Rom 8:11
> *"But if the Spirit of Him who raised Jesus from the dead dwells in you, He who raised Christ Jesus from the dead will also give life to your mortal bodies through His Spirit who dwells in you."*

"But" refers to the alternative lifestyle that is available and we now have a better choice. "If" refers to the conditions we are required to fulfill so that we can reverse the process and its outcomes.

But if we allow the Holy Spirit to dwell within us in full measure, He will give life to our mortal body and quicken it with life. Thus, our physical body can rejuvenate itself into strength and vitality.

> Ps 103:5
> *"Who satisfies your years with good things, So that your youth is renewed like the eagle."*

When our body is quickened with new strength and life, our life is extended. We move further away from the grave as God prolongs our lives. We are getting further and further from our appointment with death and live longer to testify of His goodness.

> Rom 8:2
> *"For the law of the Spirit of life in Christ Jesus has set you free from the law of sin and of death."*

The law of the Spirit of life will set us free from the law of sin and death as we set our mind on the things of the Holy Spirit. The mind must think on the things of the Holy Spirit and yield to its workings. When the mind is set in this manner, there is life and peace. It will help us to live a life pleasing to God. There will not be an enmity between God and us. We will break free from any sin that can beset us.

Rom 8:15
"For you have not received a spirit of slavery leading to fear again, but you have received a spirit of adoption as sons by which we cry out, 'Abba! Father!'"

We can be led by the Holy Spirit and be brought closer to the spirit of adoption. We can break free from the spirit of slavery that can lead us to fear again. We can be free from this spirit of slavery that can keep us in bondage to the enemy.

Heb 2:14-15
"Therefore, since the children share in flesh and blood, He Himself likewise also partook of the same, that through death He might render powerless him who had the power of death, that is, the devil, and might free those who through fear of death were subject to slavery all their lives."

God will render Satan powerless in our lives by releasing us to walk in the resurrection life. He will set us free from the fear of death because He now has given us an option to allow the Holy Spirit to quicken our mortal body so that life rejuvenates us daily. Thus breaking the cycle of death in us.

Ps 79:11
"Let the groaning of the prisoner come before You; According to the greatness of Your power preserve those who are doomed to die."

God will cancel our appointment with death and give us a new lease of life. We can live life more abundantly now. The decrees of the devil do not work upon us. They have been nullified and brought to nothing.

They Are A People Movement for Kingdom Advancement

Ps 102:22
"When the peoples are gathered together, And the kingdoms, to serve the LORD."

The proceeding word is clear that when this finishing generation gathers together and becomes accurately connected, their synergy will accelerate the advancement of the Kingdom of God here on the earth.

The Holy Spirit is currently connecting together the lives of these men who have the same DNA all across the earth. There is a people movement that is gathering momentum together. These men are like brothers of the same family and tribe who are strengthening each other so that our rising is enhanced.

Ps 133:1-3
"A Song of Ascents, of David. Behold, how good and how pleasant it is For brothers to dwell together in unity! It is like the precious oil upon the head, Coming down upon the beard, Even Aaron's beard, Coming down upon the edge of his robes. It is like the dew of Hermon Coming down upon the mountains of Zion; For there the LORD commanded the blessing--life forever."

The "brothers" in these verses refer to the same family of Aaron. The priestly anointing oil cannot be placed on another person other than a priest. Thus the oil will be demanded on all those who are connecting to Aaron. There is a pressure placed upon the hearers to supply fresh oil on all those who are accurately connected. God will command the blessings into that place, and life forevermore.

When the accurate connecting is established, the synergy will multiply strength for the whole body to move forward in Kingdom advancement. Then the nations

of the world will become the Kingdom of Christ and He will reign forever.

The coming together of this finishing generation will force the spirit of darkness to depart from all our territories. The enemy of our soul will never be able to ford us within our walls. He will not resist our movement anymore. When we come together and are covenanted together we wield a powerful strength before our enemies. The enhanced strength, when fathers and sons are connected together in an honorable way, is strategic. We will be able to put the enemies out of our territories.

> Ps 127:5
> *"How blessed is the man whose quiver is full of them; They will not be ashamed When they speak with their enemies in the gate."*

We need not be ashamed of meeting the enemies at the gates as they will never be able to resist us as we team up together as father and sons. There are so many things that will crumble as we seriously join our hearts and lives together in Kingdom advancement.

> Eph 3:18-20
> *"may be able to comprehend with all the saints what is the breadth and length and height and depth, and to know the love of Christ which surpasses knowledge, that you may be filled up to all the fullness of God. Now to Him who is able to do far more abundantly beyond all that we ask or think, according to the power that works within us,"*

When we are covenanted and connected in this family we are able to comprehend with all the saints what the breath and length and height and depth is. We can give structure and dimensions to that which is spiritual. Then we will be able to see the God who is able to do far more abundantly beyond all that we ask or think, in full demonstration. This finishing generation will rise to reveal a new measure of grace which they possess as sons of God. Their rising will bring kings and nations to their knees. This finishing generation will be able to bring to a close the curtain of time on prophetic fulfillment so that nations will come to what is being displayed in glory.

Is 60:1-3

"Arise, shine; for your light has come, And the glory of the LORD has risen upon you. For behold, darkness will cover the earth And deep darkness the peoples; But the LORD will rise upon you And His glory will appear upon you. Nations will come to your light, And kings to the brightness of your rising.'

This new generation is rising powerfully on the new horizons of time. Get ready to march in step with what God is doing in the earth. A generation of breakthrough believers are on the rise on the earth. This is the mature generation that will bring God's word into full reality. God is raising these breakthrough believers to become world changers and city takers. The Holy Spirit will be rewarding those who labour faithfully, as they will see the fruits of their labor. God will use this generation to impact the city and influence the nation.

Let us discover how these breakthrough believers can be raised and released. We must empower and appoint them to finish their assignment here on earth.

Chapter Three

The Finishing Generation Of Breakthrough Believers

We begin our apostolic foundation laying by raising the right kind of people for the right kind of job. We need to raise breakthrough believers who possess a prevailing mentality to advance the kingdom. The church will take the shape of the type of people it houses. The attitude of the people determines how much work is going to be done.

The quality of the hearts of the people will determine how far they go in finishing the call of God for their lives. The governing church is commissioned to produce breakthrough believers. In fact, without God raising breakthrough believers, governing churches will cease to exist. Breakthrough believers make it possible for governing churches to emerge.

Definition Of A Breakthrough Believer

A breakthrough believer is an extraordinary par excellence believer with a prevailing kingdom mentality and a Christ-likeness in expression of character rising progressively to his God-given potential and calling

that is now being used to create influence and impact upon those around him for the purpose of kingdom advancement.

The breakthrough believer is not from an elite company, but a believer who is extraordinary. He is distinguished among others because he carries a spirit of excellence in all that he does and in all that he is. This prevailing mindset sets him apart as a unique distinctive individual. He has a sound mind that allows him to view all things victoriously from a prevailing paradigm. He thinks like a victor and not like a victim. He is pleasant to have around as he is always buoyant in his spirit carrying hope, joy and courage knowing that all things will be well in God.

This is what makes a believer a breakthrough believer; distinctively different from a breakdown believer! The quality of his thoughts, the confidence of his trust in God, the assurance of his reasoning and the courage of his decisions all make him valuable to the kingdom and to any church!

Breakthrough believers are exemplary in their expression of Christ-likeness in character. They model the kingdom lifestyle with wholeness of character. They have learned the power to live in the Spirit and put to death the deeds of the flesh. They have chosen to allow God-life to permeate through all their dealings with men. They die daily to the flesh so that others may receive life in their contact with them.

In their pursuit to be a blessing to the church, they labour in the grace of God given them to rise to their full potential and calling. They desire to excel and use everything God has entrusted them with, to be a source of blessing to others. They live to be a source of influence on all others until kingdom government is established all around them.

God uses choice instruments like these to impact the lives of others. These strategic believers create significant moves of God in their locality because they are pliable and yielded to the Holy Spirit.

The church has to produce this company of extraordinary believers so that the moves of the Holy Spirit can be advanced to reach the nations. The sooner we

produce extraordinary believers of this nature, the sooner an apostolic base will emerge in the city. When we have raised a core company of breakthrough believers, the others who come into our churches will follow the standard of life and doctrine already set by these believers. It will raise the standard of Christian expression in our city.

Men of this calibre will remove the reproach which the church has been living under for so long. They will put a new face to the church. The world will view the church in a totally different light opposed to how they are seeing us now.

The Lord will be glorified in their lifestyles. With the favour of His Presence, He will be there to confirm everything they are doing in His will. This new breed without greed will be that new type of people the Bible says, *"...yet to be created."* As we see in *Psalms 102,* When they emerge on the scene all across the earth, the kingdoms of the world will serve the Lord.

Chapter Four

Governing Principles For Raising Breakthrough Believers

Part I

There are no shortcuts in raising the best. Endeavouring to reproduce an apostolic company of believers, when we give the most time to the best of our people, the Lord will give us wisdom to bring it into reality. Apostolic wisdom can be imparted into our hearts so that we can develop accuracy in our reproducing of these "sons of the kingdom."

There are some major principles governing the process of raising these believers. When we follow these steps, we will see a new generation of believers in our churches.

Developing And Training People In Kingdom Principles And Lifestyle

This principle helps us understand that training and development are two different matters. We develop people by nurturing what they already possess and help bring it to full maturity, usage and maximum results. We develop the giftings God has put within them by activating them and coaching them to effectiveness. We develop their character and personality so that they can bring forth their gifts, talents and grace in wholesome living and expression.

We train them, however, by putting skills, patterns and accurate procedures into their lives so that they can carry out their role functions effectively. These times of training will help them become peak performers in what they are expected to do. They will produce a better work output than those who are untrained. They will then find fulfilment in their work. By developing the person, he becomes effective, but by training the person, his work becomes efficient!

We need to develop and train all our believers in kingdom principles and lifestyles. Believers are born into the kingdom of God and not into the church. Being born into the kingdom they are commanded to live under total subjection to the kingdom laws and principles.

The book of *Matthew* deals with Christ as king. The various aspects of the kingdom are adequately dealt with in this Gospel. If we read *Matthew 5, 6* and *7,* we can see some major laws of the kingdom expounded by Jesus at the mount. The "Sermon on the Mount", as it is commonly called, lays kingdom principles as foundation for kingdom lifestyle. Those who live by these principles will express the king in their character likeness.

The inability of pastors to train people to live the kingdom lifestyle, constitutes the basic problem in the church. If a man practices these principles, he "will be sons of your Father in heaven."

> Matthew 5:45
> *"so that you may be sons of your Father who is in heaven..."*

> Matthew 5:48
> *"Therefore you are to be perfect, as your heavenly Father is perfect."*

Believers must be trained to live the kingdom lifestyle so that the Father is glorified and honoured. Much of these lifestyle principles allow God to build into our lives His nature, His desires and His dealings. This pattern is to be produced in us so that we may represent Him fully. People will glorify our Father by the way we live.

> Matthew 5:16
> *"Let your light shine before men in such a way that they may see your good works, and glorify your Father who is in heaven."*

God will reward us by the way we practice righteousness in our lives. God wants us to come into a place of intimacy with Him and shut the door on every other thing. He wants to meet us and touch all our needs. He wants us to develop His nature of forgiveness in our hearts so that we can rule and reign with Him with a pure heart.

> Matthew 6:1
> *"Beware of practicing your righteousness before men to be noticed by them; otherwise you have no reward with your Father who is in heaven."*

> Matthew 6:8
> *"So do not be like them; for your Father knows what you need before you ask Him."*

> Matthew 5:8
> *"Blessed are the pure in heart, for they shall see God."*

> Matthew 6:14-15
> *"For if you forgive others for their transgressions, your heavenly Father will also forgive you. But if you do not forgive others, then your Father will not forgive your transgressions."*

The Father wants us to "seek first the kingdom and all His righteousness, then all these things which the heathen seek will be added unto us" *(Matthew 6:33).* He wants to train us to do His will so that the spirit of lawlessness will not be within our lives. We are commanded to hear His Words and act on it so that we will be like a house that cannot be shaken.

There are enough principles for accurate training of lifestyles and development of character in these three chapters of *Matthew*. Every believer must live by kingdom rules, not just church traditions and customs.

If a person learns forgiveness by living the kingdom lifestyle, he will not be carrying unforgiveness inside the church. If he has learned the kingdom lifestyle by subduing the spirit of lust, he will not be living in adultery in the church. Only those trained in kingdom living and have developed kingdom character are added to the Church.

The Church is the "Ecclesia of God" called out from the kingdom of God for a specialized task of extending and advancing the kingdom of God. The Church is that elite special force that will bring the kingdom authority and government into the earth.

When the church is filled with those who are not living the kingdom lifestyle, it ceases to have the authority to represent Him in power and authority. The church today is weak and anaemic because it is filled with people who know nothing about kingdom living and kingdom values. Many of those moving in leadership do not possess an exemplary kingdom lifestyle but have the lifestyle that only fits into an institutional church role function. Thus they will only reproduce after their kind and after what they have become. We can have thousands of those who are not trained in the kingdom lifestyle in our churches, but they will not be able to help the church create impact on our community. They do not possess the distinctive kingdom qualities that will make them the light and salt of the earth! They will not be able to make the difference!

Making People Wholesome In All Aspects Of Life To Manifest Christ-Likeness

Mark 1:17
"And Jesus said to them, "Follow Me, and I will make you become fishers of men."

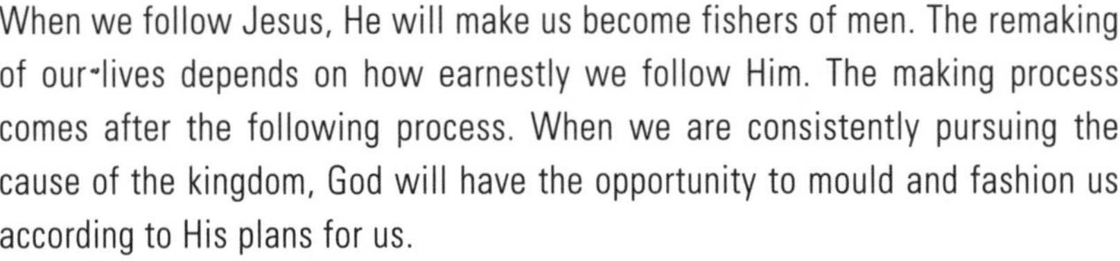

When we follow Jesus, He will make us become fishers of men. The remaking of our lives depends on how earnestly we follow Him. The making process comes after the following process. When we are consistently pursuing the cause of the kingdom, God will have the opportunity to mould and fashion us according to His plans for us.

As we desire to raise breakthrough believers, we must be prepared to bring changes into the lives of those whom we are leading. We need to demand change, not only suggest change. A leader leads and does not allow people to walk in indecisiveness because "a wavering mind receives nothing from God." These indecisive people will weaken the frontlines of kingdom advancement and will bring the work into a vulnerable position before the enemies.

All the believers in our churches must be wholesome in the areas of their manhood or womanhood. This is the true foundation of all ministries in the kingdom. We are doomed to a humiliating collapse if we fail to build our ministries on a solid base of personal purity and maturity. Clean hands and clean hearts results in a clean walk in holiness.

Man was first made in His image and likeness before he was given a "ministry" in the garden. Jesus learnt obedience for thirty years before the Holy Spirit came in fullness over Him. God wants to bring every child into sonship and the process of maturity to manhood is very essential. We must be able to bring all our believers into this process of maturity to manhood.

There are a few specific areas that seal maturity into manhood. They are in the areas of marriage, motive, morality and money.

A. Marriage

The area of marriage is a critical area that deserves our immediate attention. Marriage must reflect the relationship of Jesus and the Church *(Ephesians 5:22-23)*. The kind of relationship that must permeate from all the activities of a husband and wife together as one, is a relationship of sacrifice, honour and submission. Our spouses should be our best friends and companions in

our lives' journey. No one else should find that place of closeness with us emotionally or mentally.

> Ephesians 5:22-23
> *"Wives, be subject to your own husbands, as to the Lord. For the husband is the head of the wife, as Christ also is the head of the church, He Himself being the Savior of the body."*

To give an occasion or room for such an advance will open the pathway for an immoral lifestyle of flirting, emotional adultery or sexual acts itself. The believers must be well disciplined in their marriages and well nourished with every spiritual help they can get to raise the standard in this corrupt world where life together in holy matrimony is ridiculed by the media and world systems. We must have a conviction of steel that ministry is not complete or wholesome if the family is not in order.

We must be taught that God's ways are to be our priority and that marriage and family forms the basic foundation for all the other activities on the earth, including our jobs, investments or businesses. To keep this order we must simply and courageously draw a line and decide; these things threatening to encroach on our family life must stop! God can't entrust His Bride to us when we can't even take care of our own!

B. Motive

The next area worthy of our attention is our motive. The reason why we do what we do is more important than the doing itself. The quality of the reason purifies the actions taken. We must discern the hidden motives of the heart so that we ourselves are not judged.

> 1 Corinthians 11:31
> *"But if we judged ourselves rightly, we would not be judged."*

We judge our own hearts by allowing the sharp two edged sword of God's Word to discern its motives and expose our hearts before us. We can see all

things clearly as He sees and judges the motives within our hearts, before they can find expression in our words and action.

> Hebrews 4:12
> *"For the word of God is living and active and sharper than any two-edged sword, and piercing as far as the division of soul and spirit, of both joints and marrow, and able to judge the thoughts and intentions of the heart."*

Most of us start life pursuing things with unclean motives and hidden agendas. When we allow the light of God's revelation to shine into our spirits and minds, we will be able to discern our own hearts. When we receive from the Holy Spirit, we receive truth which will enable us to deal with every contrary interest or hidden agenda in our hearts.

> 1 John 3:19-22
> *"We will know by this that we are of the truth, and will assure our heart before Him in whatever our heart condemns us; for God is greater than our heart and knows all things. Beloved, if our heart does not condemn us, we have confidence before God; and whatever we ask we receive from Him, because we keep His commandments and do the things that are pleasing in His sight."*

When we walk in the light the Holy Spirit has given us, we will not stumble. We can assure our hearts before Him and know that we are of the truth. We can have the confidence before God and our hearts (our spirits) will not condemn us. But if we violate our conscience, our spirit will set off the alarm that we are displeasing in His sight and not keeping His commandments. When we violate our conscience we will walk out of light into darkness and there will not be a covering of blood in that area. That area will then become vulnerable to demonic attacks.

The light God gives to us can keep the heart pure and bring us into a pure walk of devotion to Him. Our hearts will always speak to us if we violate our conscience. The ability to discern and know when our hearts condemn us, is God's way of calling us to our spirit senses so that we can come into

repentance and walk into righteousness before Him.

C. Morality

The next area that affects our maturity into manhood is in the area of our morality. The ability to live uprightly with high values of ethics and honest dealings with fellow human beings, will lead us into maturity of Christ-likeness. This issue of morality does not confine itself to sexuality but to all dealings with others. It applies to all our behaviour patterns and conduct with the opposite sex, our working colleagues, our business partners or clients. It applies to everyone we come in contact with during our walk here on this earth whether it be a Christian or a non-Christian. The high values we place on honesty, integrity, purity, peace, dependability etc. will reveal the strength of our morality.

These core values are often neglected and other non-essential characteristics are often over emphasised. The ability to preach, sing or lead takes pre-eminence over the eternal core values which make a person pleasant and likeable.

> Proverbs 19:22
> *"What is desirable in a man is his kindness, and it is better to be a poor man than a liar."*

There are only a few good men around; those who are models and champions of a wholesome life. People love them and honour them with praises. So many ministries have fallen short of these core values that would have made them endeared to others.

The standards of morality have come down so low, even among ministries today, that it is shocking. The purity of honest business dealings are only stories of the past. The purity of clean wholesome relationships with the opposite sexes is near impossible even in the church. If these core kingdom values cannot be established within the context of apostolic church believers, then concepts of covenant relationships, apostolic fathering, laying down our lives for one another and kingdom community living and corporate destinies will all be impossible to implement.

There is so much resistance to these teachings because we have not raised up the company of breakthrough believers who thrive on integrity, honesty and other kingdom values. When will the church be able to see the demonstration of the covenant that Jonathan had with David? When will we able to see the strength of the covenant relationship a Gentile woman Ruth, had with her mother-in-law Naomi? When will we see loyalty and deep commitment to arrowhead leadership like we saw in the lives of David's mighty men?

We desperately need to raise up breakthrough believers who are wholesome in all aspects of their lives. In their business dealings and in all their other relationships and friendships; they must be above board. They must walk in honesty before the income tax departments and others that they owe. Their moral fibre must be etched upon kingdom values.

D. Money

The next aspect that will affect our maturity into manhood is in the area of money. God is raising a new generation of believers who have overcome the love for this world. They have overcome the cares of this world and the deceitfulness of riches so that they can rise as a new breed without greed.

> Mark 4:19
> *"but the worries of the world, and the deceitfulness of riches, and the desires for other things enter in and choke the word, and it becomes unfruitful."*

Breakthrough believers will not be able to rise in maturity to manhood and reveal Christ-likeness in character until this love for money is rooted out from their heart and soul. Breakthrough believers need to have the love of the Father dwelling in their hearts so that they find the grace to overcome the love of the world.

In *2 Timothy 3:1-5*, we read Paul's warning that there will be six types of lovers in the last days. Lovers of self *(v. 2)*, lovers of money *(v. 2)*, lovers of violence *(v. 3)*, lovers of religion *(v. 5)*, lovers of pleasure *(v. 4)* and lovers of knowledge *(v. 7)*.

Those who are lovers of self have total disregard for relationships and the interests of others. Those who are lovers of money have total disregard for morality and ethics. Those who are lovers of violence have total disregard for life and peace. Those who are lovers of pleasure have total disregard for kingdom lifestyles and values. Those who are lovers of religion have total disregard for the fresh move of God. Those who are lovers of knowledge have total disregard for obedience as they choose to live in deception.

The love for money is the root of all evil *(1 Timothy 6:10)*. If this is the root of all evil, why are pastors not cutting it out effectively? Instead, we hear messages that entice and fan the flames of greed in the believers. *Luke 6:38, "Give and it shall be given to you ...."* is a verse often used as an encouragement during the offering time in the church service. However, this verse does not address the issue of money but mercy, compassion and forgiveness. The context of Jesus' message was on human relationship of forgiveness, mercy and peaceable behaviour. Though any Scripture can be used as an implied principle, the contextual point is not about money. There are other Scriptures that relate directly with money. As my dear friend, Dr.Tunde Bakare, says *"We have read our greed into the creed!"*

This is the reason why churches have difficulty raising finances because we have enticed people's greed rather than promote the spirit of giving and sacrifice. Every breakthrough believer must break through in their area of giving and receiving. Their financial integrity must be above board. They must learn to honour God in all their financial dealings with others. The areas of the repayment of loans must be girded with honesty. The areas of spending must be girded with wisdom. The areas of borrowing must be controlled by kingdom priorities.

Believers must be taught to divide their income into three portions. The first portion is our "tithes" which is ten percent of our income. People ask me if it's the gross or net income. The issue is not on the above, but on honour. If we give the gross now, then we would not have to give again when we cash out our provident fund or other aspects of our insurances, etc. in the future.

The second portion is called "bread." This is the amount of money we need to sustain our lifestyle.

> 2 Corinthians 9:10
> *"Now He who supplies seed to the sower and bread for food will supply and multiply your seed for sowing and increase the harvest of your righteousness... ..."*

If we live a lifestyle of debt and repayment, we will need a large bread loaf! We must learn to live below our means not just within our means. When we live within our means we live barely from hand to mouth. When we live below our means, we will have some cash left over for savings and for enough seed for sowing to reap a harvest in the future. This area is where most believers fail miserably. They buy too much, too soon on credit and acquire massive debts. This burden weighs over their lives each month and accumulates whenever they fail to service their loans and make adequate payments. The "buy first, pay later" scheme often entices believers to own things they have no capacity to have.

This forces them to desire to enjoy the luxury without paying the price. It's like choosing to have premarital sex before marriage and live in a promiscuous lifestyle. It is true, we'll be married later, but by violating a divine principle we open the door for demonic attacks not only on our testimony but also on our future married life.

Do not choose to own anything we do not need and cannot afford. Even if we can afford an item, it does not mean we should choose to have it. We must exercise total discipline of the will, a clear conscience and kingdom priority to guide each and every decision. We cannot buy everything we can afford, for then we will live in arrogance and self indulgence.

We cannot buy everything we want either, as that will lead to ill-discipline and an irresponsible lifestyle. We cannot accommodate any lifestyle that violates kingdom values and godliness. God will speak into each one of our lives the privileges and luxuries He allows for us to have. To some He gives a greater measure, to others He leads them on the straight and narrow. We are not to judge others in what they do, but rather judge our own selves so that we can be pleasing in His sight.

The last portion of our money is our "seed" for sowing. The seed is for sowing into the kingdom so that we can reap a financial harvest. In this portion, we can have seed for sowing into offerings for kingdom extension and advancement. We can also have seed for multiplication through savings or investments.

> 2 Corinthians 9:6
> *"Now this I say, he who sows sparingly will also reap sparingly, and he who sows bountifully will also reap bountifully."*

The seed for sowing will bring us a financial harvest. We must learn to sow accurately so that we will receive a consistent ongoing harvest. By operating in the principles of sowing and reaping, we can ensure a consistent ongoing supply of resources. If we sow consistently, we will also reap consistently. If we observe the laws of the harvest and act accordingly, then we will have a harvest. The sower must not sow into a ground with termites as he will not have a harvest. He cannot sow with greed so that he can get more and more. God is not into gambling where people who give little, expect to receive a jackpot! We cannot give to gain attention or gain control over the lives to whom we have given.

We learn to sow with joy now, because we have learnt to sow in tears before and have reaped a harvest. We cannot be a cheerful giver without first knowing the tearful side of kingdom sacrifice and demand. When we have learned to yield to God's demand of love, and fulfil His requirements on us, we will learn the cheerful part of seeing His abundance.

The sower of the seed must use money to multiply money. Keeping it in the bank only earns us interest. This is the minimum we can do with our money.

> Luke 19:23
> *"Then why did you not put my money in the bank, and having come, I would have collected it with interest?"*

A Savings Account allows us to have cash at our disposal. This is the short term "keep it in the bank until I need it" scheme. It is available at the point of need.

An investment does not allow us that kind of freedom as it needs to be in the pipeline for a period of time before it yields its harvest. We can only make investments if we do not need this money immediately and can spare the resources for investments.

We advise teenage believers to give 10% for tithe, 10% for offerings and keep 10% more for savings or investment each month. We encourage them to live on the seventy percent of their income. We advise students and young couples to move a step higher by living on sixty percent of their income. They are advised to develop a financial planning that consists of 10% tithe, 10% offerings, 10% savings and 10% investments. God will bless those who are willing to pay the price for kingdom lifestyle and a better future. This would be a wonderful formula if we are just starting out in life, we can do things the right way with accuracy.

We must lead all breakthrough believers into the maturity of manhood in these areas of marriage, motive, morality and money so that they reveal Christ-likeness of character. They must become trained in all aspects of living so that we reproduce wholesome people who can become instruments for God's move in our society.

Chapter Five

GOVERNING PRINCIPLES FOR RAISING BREAKTHROUGH BELIEVERS

Part II

Discipling And Mentoring Believers At Different Levels Of Maturity And Giftings

When believers are born again and added to the kingdom, we need to move them into the process of discipleship immediately! To disciple someone we need to mould them through changing their thinking patterns so that they will devote themselves to a new pattern of behaviour and conduct, expressing the desired lifestyle.

There will not be complete discipleship without changing their thinking patterns and changing their lifestyle and conduct. Many people who are converted seldom make it to discipleship. They have merely embraced another religion. They remain the same individuals they have always been. They are now in a new environment but inwardly they are unchanged. They are like the fish that was in the pond which is now in the aquarium!

Discipleship brings about a change in their thinking patterns as we teach believers to observe and devote themselves to sound doctrine. These "dogmas" regulate their thinking patterns and help them understand clearly their life as a believer. They have chosen a new lifestyle and they now know why it must be lived in this way. We must provide clear sound doctrine so that thinking patterns are changed and lifestyles challenged to honour God.

After we have trained them to live out this dimension of discipleship we need to take them to the next level. In this level of discipleship, we teach them to observe all that God Himself has taught us. We train them to know, to say and to do that which God has given us.

> Matthew 28:19-20
> *""Go therefore and make disciples of all the nations, baptizing them in the name of the Father and the Son and the Holy Spirit, teaching them to observe all that I commanded you; and lo, I am with you always, even to the end of the age.""*

Disciples are to observe all that God has commanded the apostles to do. They are to reproduce what the apostles were doing. They are to become a mouthpiece that will speak what they have heard and seen of the apostles. Thus, discipleship is not only to regulate a person's behaviour according to what we are teaching him, but also to train someone who will be able to reproduce us in all that God is calling us to do. The apostles are to make believers into disciples of their lifestyles. The Disciples must be apostolic in nature, thinking paradigm and lifestyles. Unlike the present institutional church definition of discipleship, the apostolic perception allows us to reproduce disciples with apostolic capacities.

Thus, discipleship is not only giving them a set of doctrines to adhere to, but discipleship means to reproduce after our kind so that there will be more of those who will be observing all that God has taught the arrowhead leader.

Mentoring, on the other hand, has to do with imparting skills and styles so that the believers are able to do what they are supposed to do. We are coaching them so that they can become peak performers. We show them the more excellent way of doing things so that they will learn accurate patterns of function. They will know how to do all things well in the spirit of excellence.

There is active and passive mentoring. The believer learns from our ways and he tries to do what we are doing to the best of his current ability. This is the passive mentoring program. It requires a lot of self-initiative and a keen observation of lifestyles on the part of the disciple.

The active mentoring is designed by both parties to outwork these things over a period of time. The mentor will provide consistent help until the skill is transferred and the believer is functioning effectively. The mentoring program requires yieldedness on the part of the believer so that these skills can be crafted into his life to produce effective results.

The working out of these skills of styles and performance, presentation and other abilities into the life of the believers will take time and intense practice. There must be enough opportunities given for the believers to express and do what they are learning to follow and reproduce.

Both discipleship and mentoring are basic training concepts that must become operational within an apostolic base. There must be those whom we are discipling (covers truth and thinking paradigms) and there must be those whom we are mentoring (covers skills, styles and presentation in performance).

When believers are established in these paradigms of discipleship and mentoring, we will need to select those who will choose to go higher into the next level. The next level is on spiritual fathering and it is an important apostolic strategy for succession and continuity within the church.

Spiritual fathering is an apostolic concept for reproducing the next generation of sons to whom we can transfer our legacy and ministry. God rejected Eliezer of Damascus from inheriting what Abraham had. We cannot transfer our legacy on those who are faithful only. There are other criteria for choosing succession. God also rejected Ishmael from being Abraham's heir because he was born out of a slave woman.

There are many who have grown up in leadership in the early stages of pioneering work and they have gone through thick and thin with us, but in choosing to transfer legacy, we must go beyond the obligation factor to long-standing members who have been faithful pillars of the past.

There was a third category of people in Abraham's house and the Bible records them as being born in his house in *Genesis 14:14*. They were trained men born in his house who were able to fight wars for him. These represent faithful, loyal members who have helped us grow our churches to where we are. They have been loyal and faithful. They have stood the test of time. But in order to transfer legacy, we need to look beyond the above factors. This succession factor is so essential that it would require patience and wisdom for its accurate implementation.

There is a new generation of sons and daughters that are rising in our churches who will own the House and continue the legacy of the forefathers. It is this generation that we must reproduce in the church. God said to Abraham that his son and his heir will come forth from his own body.

> Genesis 15:4
> *"Then behold, the word of the LORD came to him, saying, "This man will not be your heir; but one who will come forth from your own body, he shall be your heir.""*

This apostolic concept of sonship is impossible to implement without the Spirit of wisdom on the arrowhead leadership. The arrowhead leader or apostle must first turn his heart towards his sons or sons to be. When our hearts are opened by the Father's love for these men, the way we minister to them will change. We will feel affectionately for their lives and destinies. There is a care and concern for them that signals a new enlarging of our hearts to them. Often it is a small company of men in the large crowd. Jesus always picked out the strategic ones in the crowd.

It is fathers who look for sons and rarely the other way around. It is the natural father who has the sense of ownership over his child even before the child recognises or understands who he is. The father changes the child's diapers and cleans him up even before he receives a thank you! The child finally opens his mouth after a few months of preferential treatment and says the first "papa" or "dada"! Fathers must be wholesome in the Father's love for them to be able to serve and minister in faith, love and patience towards those whom they will beget in the future.

Churches must move from membership to sonship mentalities. We are not promoting the idea that the pastor becomes a spiritual father immediately, as this is a process of maturity and wisdom. We cannot choose the pathway of spiritual fathering without first knowing that we ourselves have become our Heavenly Father's true son in nature and heart. Neither can we choose the pathway of spiritual fathering when the believers have never even walked the pathway of discipleship or mentoring. We cannot embark on this pathway if we have difficulty in being a regular local church pastor. We must already be effective in ministering what God is saying to the church. We must be in a spiritual stature of maturity and wholeness before we embark on this process of succession in the local church through fathering.

There are many foundations that are needed to be laid before we can choose to embrace the truth on spiritual fathering. Spiritual fathering is a legitimate restorative truth being delivered by strong apostolic men who are laying a spiritual legacy for their succeeding generation of sons.

Believers in the church must first be strongly discipled and mentored. We must build into them the inner patterns of kingdom lifestyle, the spiritual dynamics of the house and also the sense of corporate destiny into their hearts. We must then lead them to sense a deep knowing in their hearts that they are true sons of the Heavenly Father. The church, the house of God, is their Father's house and the work is the Father's business. This knowing in their hearts will open the spiritual dimensions within the church for strong apostolic grace to be endowed upon them and for the arrowhead leader to begin the process of spiritual fathering. The revelation of the fatherhood of God in the church will cause a new breed of true sons in the House to emmerge. This grace will translate itself into the relationship between the pastor of the local house and his congregation.

Cultivating A Worshipful Heart And Intense Passion For His Presence

This principle for raising breakthrough believers will allow the arrowhead leader to be surrounded by a company of people who love God and who are true worshippers in the Spirit. Those who know how to be tender in the presence of God and who are pliable to the dealings of the Holy Spirit are the safest ones to have around.

They are so yielded in their hearts that they will be our protection in times of need or confusion. They will be able to hear God and push through in the Spirit bringing deliverance in different situations. We often use other measurements when looking for a potential leader without realizing that whoever we choose who is not connected to God will connect to something else in the future! His wrong connections will contaminate the spiritual lives of those who genuinely love the presence of God and who want the depths of the things of the Spirit.

> 2 Chronicles 29:11
> *""My sons, do not be negligent now, for the LORD has chosen you to stand before Him, to minister to Him, and to be His ministers and burn incense.""*

The priests and the Levites were chosen to stand before Him and were given a place of honour in His Presence. They were chosen to minister to Him in worship and sacrifice. They were to be His ministers and become available to do what He wanted done. Out of the four descriptions of their tasks as priests, three of the above were God-ward and in service to Him. The last portion was to burn incense and minister to the people.

Seventy-five percent of the ministry is God-ward and only twenty-five percent was man-ward. If we can find pastors and leaders living in this dimension of worship and honour, we will have a better representation of God and His presence through these lives. Our lives should become channels for His grace and presence to flow through.

Those who are true worshippers are sought after by the Father. He will reveal the secrets of His heart to them as He did to David. God often releases His favour upon them to build them as an enduring house and be identified with them. Jesus was called the Son of David!

Looking at *Isaiah 6*, we can see the power of a worshipful and yielded heart. The courage to continue to move forward into the presence of God allowed Isaiah to see the provisions of God's mercy and a redefinition of God's call upon his own life.

The worshipper must not become contaminated by any earthly associations or distractions. No matter who we are connected to and have friendship with, our personal revelation of God must not be marred.

> Isaiah 6:1
> *"In the year of King Uzziah's death I saw the Lord sitting on a throne, lofty and exalted, with the train of His robe filling the temple."*

The worshipper must realize that there are others who know Him more deeply and he can be sanctified by their worship expressions.

> Isaiah 6:2-3
> *"Seraphim stood above Him, each having six wings: with two he covered his face, and with two he covered his feet, and with two he flew. And one called out to another and said, "Holy, Holy, Holy, is the LORD of hosts, the whole earth is full of His glory.""*

Sing the song of worshippers and be caught up into what they are feeling and experiencing. Follow the sound of a worshipper's heart and be blessed by the atmosphere it creates.

The worshipper must know how to discern his own spiritual state when he comes into the presence of God.

Isaiah 6:5

"Then I said, "Woe is me, for I am ruined! Because I am a man of unclean lips, And I live among a people of unclean lips; For my eyes have seen the King, the LORD of hosts.""

1 Corinthians 14:25

"...... the secrets of his heart are disclosed; and so he will fall on his face and worship God, declaring that God is certainly among you."

The worshipper must be overwhelmed by a God consciousness rather than sin consciousness. Most believers have an inability to deal with sin in the presence of God. They choose to become condemned and shy away from His presence altogether. Isaiah reached forward towards the Throne as this is the Throne of grace and not one of judgement. Believers must be taught how to approach God with righteousness, as He has the power to forgive and cleanse those who come to Him with a pure heart of repentance.

The worshipper will have access into the very core of God's desires as he has the closest place in God's heart. God reveals His desires and speaks His Word to those who are nearest to Him and who seek Him with a passionate heart.

John 4:23

"But an hour is coming, and now is, when the true worshipers will worship the Father in spirit and truth; for such people the Father seeks to be His worshipers."

Revelation 19:10

"Then I fell at his feet to worship him. But he said to me, "Do not do that; I am a fellow servant of yours and your brethren who hold the testimony of Jesus; worship God. For the testimony of Jesus is the spirit of prophecy.""

It's only the company of those who worship God that hear clearly the testimony of Jesus. The prophetic sound of His voice is for those who carry His heart in worship!

Finally, worshippers know that the true power of success is in the act of total

obedience. Isaiah had to know that true success is not the glamour and hype of human activities. In fact, God told him that everything and everyone will be shaken. Nothing is going to be left unturned and unshaken.

God has commanded him to speak and prophesy until revival comes. But when he spoke, a shaking took place and he saw that there was no natural success anywhere around him. The discouraged prophet asked God how long will he keep speaking and prophesying before he sees revival. God told him that everything that is not of Him will be removed as Isaiah speaks into the spirit realm. Though in the natural he only saw the negatives, God is bringing a new order in the chaos. God was doing a work beyond the natural sight and He was establishing a new core of breakthrough believers ou of whom He will raise up a holy nation. The Holy Seed will sprout again and God will bring about what He has said.

When we train every believer to cultivate a worshipful heart, the atmosphere will be conducive for a fresh move of the Spirit in our churches. God will cleanse the hearts of the people and raise a new breed upon whose shoulders the Ark of God will rest.

Chapter Six

Governing Principles For Raising Breakthrough Believers

Part III

Honouring Covenant Relationships In Marriage, Family, Ministry Team And Church Life

Every breakthrough believer in the apostolic base must be trained to honour the bonds of covenant that exists within relationships ordained and joined by God. There are very little honour, integrity, loyalty and commitment to any form of long-term relationships in the world. Actually, there is no honor among thieves!

> 1 Timothy 4:3
> *"… …men who forbid marriage and advocate abstaining from foods which God has created to be gratefully shared in by those who believe and know the truth."*

Those who are walking in sin, deception and hypocrisy will reject any loyalty, commitment and integrity in any long-term relationships in life. Those who

choose to walk in the flesh and who are lovers of self and pleasure prefer "to squander his estate in loose living" *(Luke 15:13)*.

Whenever we choose wholesome a relationship, we will have to change our thinking patterns to accommodate and please the one we are relating to. Selfishness destroys relationship. Undue expression of self can offend others in a relationship and sow discord among those whom God is bringing together.

We must give value to all God-ordained relationships, be it between Christians or otherwise. There are no two standards for relationships. In fact the relationship between Christians should go beyond the basic righteousness of man and operate on divine principles. We must take it to the next level.

Marriage is a covenant not a contract. It does not operate as a partnership between two people who mutually bless each other. These reciprocal benefits can hold a marriage relationship together but the force to hold the couple together will become weaker over the years. Mum Helen and I have known each other for over twenty-seven years and it gets better and stronger each year. When we understand the nature and spirit of covenant, we can see how it will protect us from the corruption that is in the world by lust *(2 Peter 1:4)*.

God is the God of covenant and all His dealings with mankind have been on the basis of covenant. Every promise in the Bible and every requirement of the believer is based on the grounds of covenant. In covenant living with God, He is bound to honour His Words and we are duty bound to maintain our part of the covenant.

> Genesis 15:8
> *"He said, 'O Lord GOD, how may I know that I will possess it?'"*

This is the age old question every believer is asking. God told Abraham to cut a covenant with Him. God promised Abraham that the covenant He will make with him is not nullified even if Abraham dies. It will be continued towards Abraham's descendants. God promised that He would look after his descendants and punish those who will oppress them. He will take personal responsibility to fulfil every word of promise even after Abraham's death *(Genesis 15:13-16)*.

In establishing an understanding among the believers of the power of a covenant with God, we are laying strong foundations for other wholesome relationships within the house. The beneficiary of any covenant relationship is the next generation.

> Malachi 2:14-15
> *"Yet you say, 'For what reason?' Because the LORD has been a witness between you and the wife of your youth, against whom you have dealt treacherously, though she is your companion and your wife by covenant. But not one has done so who has a remnant of the Spirit. And what did that one do while he was seeking a godly offspring? Take heed then to your spirit, and let no one deal treacherously against the wife of your youth."*

God is interested in the holy seed, a godly offspring coming forth in the covenant relationship of marriage. If we have the measures of the Holy Spirit we will not act treacherously in our covenant relationship because it was destined to bring forth a new generation. The covenant God made with every strategic man in the Bible also benefited the next generation. When we live within the context of covenant we can tap into the abundance of God's provision, protection and favour.

> Matthew 15:26-28
> *"And He answered and said, 'It is not good to take the children's bread and throw it to the dogs.' But she said, 'Yes, Lord; but even the dogs feed on the crumbs which fall from their masters' table.' Then Jesus said to her, 'O woman, your faith is great; it shall be done for you as you wish.' And her daughter was healed at once."*

There are blessings we cannot receive until we are part of God's covenant. Even though faith allows us to find access into the partial benefits of this covenant, it is a covenanted life that gives us the full privilege as a son of the covenant. There are so many of those who "operate in faith" and have tapped into the blessings of the covenant. What they do not realize is that they are only receiving the crumbs which fall from the master's table.

These people who do not live a life of covenant with God are able to receive and have their needs met, but this is only a dog's life! If we can choose to walk in covenant, we can partake of the bread on the master's table and live like sons! Many of those operating in faith outside of a covenanted lifestyle of faith will only get the crumbs of God's provision. God wants us to walk into a covenant lifestyle and enjoy the benefits of a covenant with better promises.

If we choose to live in abundance and the fullness of His favour, we must be part of the Master's House and be in covenant. These benefits accorded are superior and significant in relation to the crumbs others have chosen to eat.

> Ephesians 1:3
> *"Blessed be the God and Father of our Lord Jesus Christ, who has blessed us with every spiritual blessing in the heavenly places in Christ,..."*

There are blessings of the Father and the blessings of God. The blessings of God is seen when the sun shines on the righteous as well as the wicked. The rain falls on the righteous as well as the wicked. However, the blessings of the Father are only reserved for His sons and they will receive all that He is gathering for them and all that He has.

> Genesis 25:5-6
> *"Now Abraham gave all that he had to Isaac; but to the sons of his concubines, Abraham gave gifts while he was still living, and sent them away from his son Isaac eastward, to the land of the east."*

Isaac, the son received all. The "sons of the concubines" will only have gifts, ministries, etc. and will be sent far away from the son. Those who choose to walk in meaningful covenant relationship within the church will greatly benefit from their future inheritance.

1 Samuel 18:3-4

"Then Jonathan made a covenant with David because he loved him as himself. Jonathan stripped himself of the robe that was on him and gave it to David, with his armor, including his sword and his bow and his belt."

The one thing that Jonathan failed to give David was his shoes. When David went to the caves of Engedi, Jonathan chose to return to his father's palace. Jonathan could have lived longer if he had stayed where the covenant of God was. God's Word and covenant was with David and not Saul. Covenant relationships are incomplete if we choose different destinies in life.

Amos 3:3

"Do two men walk together unless they have made an appointment?"

Ruth chose to be in covenant with her mother-in-law, Naomi. She chose to leave Moab and return to Judah with her. Her choice of covenant opened up for her a brand new future with Boaz. The decision to pursue covenant in God will only result in a better and more meaningful future.

David's covenant with Jonathan affected his next generation. Jonathan's son, Mephibosheth, became the beneficiary of the covenant blessing.

2 Samuel 9:1

"Then David said, 'Is there yet anyone left of the house of Saul, that I may show him kindness for Jonathan's sake?'"

2 Samuel 9:3

"The king said, 'Is there not yet anyone of the house of Saul to whom I may show the kindness of God?' And Ziba said to the king, 'There is still a son of Jonathan who is crippled in both feet.'"

2 Samuel 9:7

"David said to him, 'Do not fear, for I will surely show kindness to you for the sake of your father Jonathan, and will restore to you all the land of your grandfather Saul; and you shall eat at my table regularly.'"

2 Samuel 9:13
"So Mephibosheth lived in Jerusalem, for he ate at the king's table regularly. Now he was lame in both feet."

David showed kindness to Mephibosheth for Jonathan's sake. He ate regularly at the king's table. The prophetic warning that must prevail within our hearts is that whatever we leave incomplete in our covenant with someone will be the area of conflict and defeat in the next generation. Jonathan did not give up his shoes and the next generation was crippled in both feet!

Our insufficient commitment and loyalty to covenant today can jeopardize the destiny of our next generation. David protected Mephibosheth from being killed when the Gibeonites wanted to avenge the attacks of Saul upon them when he violated a covenant previously made with them. It was the covenant Jonathan made with David that protected his son from being a casualty in the hands of the Gibeonites.

2 Samuel 21:7
"But the king spared Mephibosheth, the son of Jonathan the son of Saul, because of the oath of the LORD which was between them, between David and Saul's son Jonathan."

We must teach the believers to honour covenant within marriage and within all relationships God has ordained for our lives together in destiny.

Psalm 133:1
"Behold, how good and how pleasant it is for brothers to dwell together in unity!"

The Hebrew word for brothers is "adelphoi" and it means "brothers from the same father or brothers from the same womb." We can see that those who are in covenant are entitled to inherit the same grace and anointing.

In *Psalm 133:2,* the precious oil and the priestly anointing that flowed upon Aaron also flowed down to all his sons. When brothers are connected together in covenant and they choose to dwell together in corporate destiny, it puts pressure upon the heavens to send the oil down upon the whole body. The church believers must be instructed to put pressure upon the oil of heaven to fall afresh by our dwelling and living together in covenant community. There the Lord will command the blessings and life forevermore.

When the church in the book of *Acts* grew into a covenant community of believers, the supernatural manifestation of power began to be made manifest.

> Acts 2:42-45
> *"They were continually devoting themselves to the apostles' teaching and to fellowship, to the breaking of bread and to prayer. Everyone kept feeling a sense of awe; and many wonders and signs were taking place through the apostles. And all those who had believed were together and had all things in common; and they began selling their property and possessions and were sharing them with all, as anyone might have need."*

This covenant community modelled the kingdom lifestyle that revealed the true reformation of the society. Believers were selling their land, which for every Jew was his inheritance for the future generation. We cannot separate Jews from land and land from the Jews, yet, when true reformation of values took place in their hearts, they chose a covenant community living of a different kind. There were people being added to this company day by day *(Acts 2:47).*

Believers must be taught to honour these aspects of covenant so that they will honour all relationships God brings them into.

> Matthew 1:23-25
> *"'BEHOLD, THE VIRGIN SHALL BE WITH CHILD AND SHALL BEAR A SON, AND THEY SHALL CALL HIS NAME IMMANUEL,' which translated means, 'GOD WITH US.' And Joseph awoke from his sleep and did as the angel of the Lord commanded him, and took Mary as his wife, but kept her a virgin until she gave birth to a Son; and he called His name Jesus."*

Mary conceived the Child when the Holy Spirit came upon her. She was carrying in her the Son of God. The Seed within her was holy. However, this conception was "illegal" to the religious system surrounding her. If the Jews had found out that she was with child before she was married, they would have stoned her.

There are some things that God deposits in us that are illegal to the religious system. The religious environment is never favourable to the holy seed we have conceived by the Holy Spirit. This is one of the major reasons why God gives us wholesome covenant relationship. When Joseph was betrothed to Mary, he protected her from these attacks and covered her until the child was born. He did not touch her but kept her a virgin until the Son was born.

In wholesome covenant relationships, there is protection for the holy seed within our hearts. True covenant friends and fathers will not destroy the seed God has put into our lives. They will nurture the Christ within our lives until He is brought to full maturity. Joseph did not use his conjugal rights as a husband but honoured the Child and Seed of God within her. Spiritual fathers are prepared to see to the full potential of Christ-life breaking out in us. They wait patiently as a husbandman for the first fruits of the crop to be brought into harvest.

God is allowing meaningful relationships of covenant to be formed in the church today so that we will be close enough to guard the Christ in each one of us. We are to nourish and cherish the life of God within each other so that we will all reach our full potential in Christ. We are here to help one another grow into maturity "being fitted and held together by what every joint supplies, according to the proper working of each individual part, causing the growth of the whole body for the building up of itself in love" *(Ephesians 4:16)*.

Expressing Christ's Compassion To Reach The Unsaved And Meet The Needs Of The Community

This last governing principle is very essential for the raising up of breakthrough believers. Most believers have gotten so stuck into church activities that they have forgotten the real conditions in the world. Believers are so out of touch with the world after a few years in church that it is staggering.

They are in meetings everyday and have lost contact with all their past friends and acquaintances. Within a few years, they do not have any more friends outside the boundaries of the church. Every friend is someone in the church. Every function they attend is associated to the church. Every wedding is a Christian wedding; so is every funeral. The world of the believer is soon shut in and under siege.

> Matthew 9:36-38
> *"Jesus was going through all the cities and villages, teaching in their synagogues and proclaiming the gospel of the kingdom, and healing every kind of disease and every kind of sickness. Seeing the people, He felt compassion for them, because they were distressed and dispirited like sheep without a shepherd. Then He said to His disciples, 'The harvest is plentiful, but the workers are few. Therefore beseech the Lord of the harvest to send out workers into His harvest.'"*

Jesus felt compassion for the people. Compassion is the passion of Jesus compelling us to do something that Jesus Himself would do for them. Jesus saw them as being responsive to His message and to Him *(v. 35)*. Jesus saw them as being distressed and disappointed because their problems were beyond their ability to cope with and was overwhelming them. Jesus said that only true shepherds can lead them out from this state and from their needs into the reality of the Kingdom of God.

Jesus clearly defined that the harvest is already before us. He told us that the harvest field is already ripe and all that are needed are the labourers. We need labourers who can work on the people to bring them into the kingdom. Jesus did not ask us to pray for the harvest, but for labourers to go into these fields as the harvest is already plentiful.

Believers who have become very active in church work often become cut off from reaching the community. We are often cut off from feeling deeply for those outside our walls. In fact, our walls are so thick that it keeps us in and keeps them out!

The believers in the church must learn to build bridges instead of walls so that we can allow the compassion of Jesus to flow through us to touch these people. Jesus' compassion for the lost was not cut off because of His successful ministry.

Matthew 9:35
"Jesus was going through all the cities and villages, teaching in their synagogues and proclaiming the gospel of the kingdom, and healing every kind of disease and every kind of sickness."

In fact, the ongoing success of our ministry is dependent on raising true shepherds who will reach out and touch society as He would. I believe that the shepherding ministry is more than just winning souls into the kingdom. Jesus was interested in restoring the human person in totality, rather than adding him to an already decaying religious system!

God must redefine the truth of the shepherd's ministry for us. The undue expectation placed upon them has caused stress and strain on shepherds. Jesus gave clear instructions to the twelve as He sent them out to impact the region *(Matthew 10:5-15)*. We have interpreted so much of what Jesus is saying in this chapter to represent an evangelical view point of soul-winning.

Breakthrough believers must be meaningfully introduced to the true shepherding ministry so that their expectations of pastors and leaders are properly aligned to scriptural patterns rather than religious systems of operation. The believers must know some fundamental truths so that they can operate within a wholesome boundary, and proper shepherding of the flock can begin.

Firstly, sheep must be cared for and loved. One of the most wholesome anointing is the shepherding anointing. Shepherds should feel what the sheep feel. The shepherd knows the sheep by name and knows well the condition of the flock.

Proverbs 27:23
"Know well the condition of your flocks, and pay attention to your herds... ...."

Sheep need the closeness of a healthy relationship with the shepherd. People must get connected to a true shepherd in a personal way not just through his ministry but through his life. The shepherd must "go down" and relate so that the sheep can respond to the care and love shown. Believers must be encouraged to be honourable in responding to the love and care shown, so that meaningful relationships are formed within the house.

Secondly, sheep need to be fed. This is one of the most important requirements in ministry. Most shepherds equate teaching to feeding. Teaching is not feeding as we can learn many wonderful truths and still be hungry. Feeding is internal and teaching is mental. To feed them means to minister to the whole person in order to restore their lives. If the person is broken, it means we need to make him whole and complete.

If a person's personality is selfish, we need to change them to what they ought to become. It means we must take them and remould them. It means to give them all the nourishment and food until they are in the place God wants them to be.

Feeding is to make the man complete and wholesome, whereas teaching is giving them knowledge and instructions. A child can have a lot of computer lessons or skills in playing the piano, yet starve if there is no food to feed the child. The sheep need to be fed with the right kind of food.

The baby must be given the water of the Word *(Ephesians 5:26)*. This is the "foundational aspect" of his kingdom life. This young babe is taught the truths concerning the "knowledge of salvation"

The infant must be given the milk of the Word *(1 Peter 2:2, Hebrews 5:13, 1 Corinthians 3:2-3)*. This is the "devotional aspect" of his life. He understands the "effects of salvation" as he exercises his will to choose life and obedience.

The young men must be given the meat of the Word *(1 John 2:14, John 4:34, John 5:30,36)*. This is the "destiny aspect" of his life. He discovers why he has been saved and the "purpose of salvation" becomes clearly unfolded.

The father must be given the solid food of wisdom *(Hebrews 5:14, 1 Corinthians 2:6-8, 13)*. This is the "manhood aspect" of his life. He understands and experiences "maturity to manhood through salvation"

The mature fathers are given the council of the Word *(Revelation 2:17, John 6:49-51)*. This is the "communion aspect" of his life. He knows the "God of our salvation" and His fatherhood on a personal level.

True shepherds feed the flock at the right time and with the right type of food.

> Matthew 24:45
> *"Then He will answer them, "Truly I say to you, to the extent that you did not do it to one of the least of these, you did not do it to Me.""*

Thirdly, sheep must be led. In true shepherding the shepherds leading establishes some major patterns in the life of the sheep. In leading, we open the door for the sheep. We must recognize that God can use us to open the heavens for them so that they can have their breakthroughs. We can help them enter into new and greater heights. In leading we train the sheep to hear and respond to our voice.

There is a trust they must develop to the sound of our voice so that we can lead them effectively. We can train them to choose the life of obedience. We can make demands of love for obedience so that they can see results.

In leading we also set the example for others to follow. We need to go ahead of them and breakthrough before their eyes, so that they can see the pattern and pathway to go forward. They observe our lives and imitate our examples of faith.

In leading them forward, our voice will become the plumb line to discern the voice of strangers. We must teach them to draw from us as the primary source. We open the door and the sheep go in and out and find pasture. The sheep must recognize that we are their primary source for spiritual nourishment. We are a catalyst for their revival. They must learn to feed upon what we are saying as leaders, and believe it will change their lives on earth.

Acts 3:4-6

"But Peter, along with John, fixed his gaze on him and said, "Look at us!" And he began to give them his attention, expecting to receive something from them. But Peter said, "I do not possess silver and gold, but what I do have I give to you: In the name of Jesus Christ the Nazarene--walk!""

In this governing principle of expressing Christ's compassion to reach the unsaved and the community, we need to restore the ministry of the true shepherds in the House. They are the care giver of the flock. They are showers of mercy and compassion. They open the bowls of compassion for others to be blessed by its expression. God wants a new breed of believers who will rise in the compassion of God and affect others with the love of God.

Believers must be trained to become His heart and His hands to embrace, to love and to care until others are brought to wholeness in His love.

Chapter Seven

CHARACTERISTICS OF BREAKTHROUGH BELIEVERS

Isaiah 61:9

"Then their offspring will be known among the nations, and their descendants in the midst of the peoples. All who see them will recognize them because they are the offspring whom the LORD has blessed."

There are clear distinctive characteristics in breakthrough believers. They can be identified in every nation of the world. Their unique features allow them to be singled out from the masses. Those who see them will know that they are making the difference. Those who meet them will know the kingdom presence of righteousness, peace and joy in the Holy Ghost.

Acts 11:19-24

"So then those who were scattered because of the persecution that occurred in connection with Stephen made their way to Phoenicia and Cyprus and Antioch, speaking the word to no one except to Jews alone. But there were some of them, men of Cyprus and Cyrene, who came to Antioch and began speaking to the Greeks also, preaching the Lord Jesus. And the hand of the Lord was with them, and a large number who believed turned to the Lord. The news about them reached the ears of the church at Jerusalem,

and they sent Barnabas off to Antioch. Then when he arrived and witnessed the grace of God, he rejoiced and began to encourage them all with resolute heart to remain true to the Lord; for he was a good man, and full of the Holy Spirit and of faith. And considerable numbers were brought to the Lord."

In applying the governing principles mentioned in the last chapters, we will be able to raise a new breed whom the church can be built upon and the kingdom advanced through. This company is the hope of the nations when the church returns to its glory and power. These breakthrough believers reveal unique characteristics that set them apart from the normal institutional church believers. A new breed without greed is emerging across the earth. God has placed upon them unique characteristics that will set them apart to make a difference in this dying world.

Moved Ahead To Pioneer A New Move Of God

They have the ability to move ahead to pioneer a new move for kingdom advancement, breaking the barriers of culture, race and human limitations. They were not confined by the traditional boundaries of Judaism. They were prepared to break the limitations of race and culture and reach out to those outside these lines of separation. The Jews had no dealings with Samaritans or Gentiles *(John 4:9)*. The persecution of the brethren, the constant threat of those who hate the fresh moves of the Holy Spirit and the fear of being thrown into jail did not keep these breakthrough believers from moving ahead. Every pioneer will have to face the challenges of being willing to be "a seed that will fall to the ground and die alone" and then, after death has taken place, it shall bear forth much fruit.

As a pioneer we have to face the lack of role models and examples in that field we are advancing. Our motives to become instrumental in the fresh move of God and to advance it, will be purged. If we have any other agenda or passion

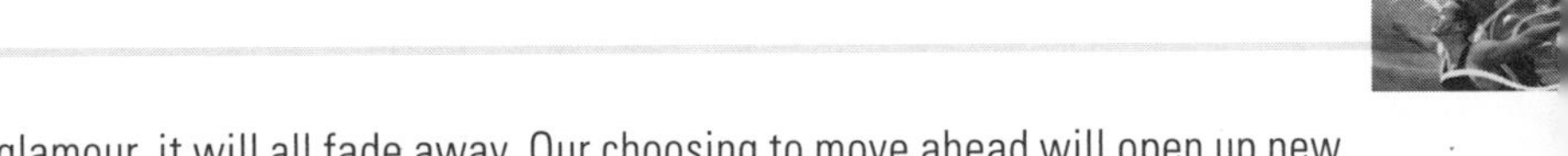

for glamour, it will all fade away. Our choosing to move ahead will open up new territories for God to impact the regions around us.

Moved Under Intense Pressure To Set The Pace

These breakthrough believers have the ability to move under intense pressure allowing God to fashion their character and raise the standard for the succeeding generation of followers. The intense persecution and the scores of martyrs did not kill the momentum and the intensity of the advancement. The pressure of the persecution produced a better quality of men for the kingdom. They were not "chocolate soldiers" who melted under the heat of the sun. The prevailing mindset and an overcoming spirit allowed the breakthrough believers to rise above the sufferings to advance the kingdom.

Breakthrough believers must be trained to push their own fears and limitations to realise their full potential in God. We have to doubt our doubts and frighten our own fears away by letting God rise within our spirits. We must be trained never to fall back, but push forward despite hardship and pressures.

We must be encouraged to die fighting, rather than die as cowards. The cowardly will turn back in the heat of the battle even though years of training and impartation has been invested in them.

> Psalm 78:9-10
> *"The sons of Ephraim were archers equipped with bows, yet they turned back in the day of battle. They did not keep the covenant of God and refused to walk in His law......."*

The sons of Ephraim had a double portion blessing of grace upon them. They were trained and skilled men of war but chose to break covenant with God when they were most needed for national victory *(v. 9)*. By not holding on to faithfulness and steadfastness, they allowed the enemy in

by breaking covenant with God. Breakthrough believers are not quitters. They do not allow the enemies to come through them to defeat Israel. They station themselves wisely so that they are always the strongest link in the chain.

> Nehemiah 4:13
> *"......then I stationed men in the lowest parts of the space behind the wall, the exposed places, and I stationed the people in families with their swords, spears and bows."*

The most exposed places are guarded by the presence of the strongest men. We must stand under the pressure to fight for the deliverance and safety of others.

> 1 Chronicles 11:13-14
> *"He was with David at Pasdammim when the Philistines were gathered together there to battle, and there was a plot of ground full of barley; and the people fled before the Philistines. They took their stand in the midst of the plot and defended it, and struck down the Philistines; and the LORD saved them by a great victory."*

God needs this company of fearless defenders of the kingdom. They defy hell and all that is against them in order to complete their mission! When these mighty men arise, the standards in the house of God will be raised. The next company of follower-ship will walk into a higher order of Kingdom living.

The stories of David's mighty men still strike awe in our hearts because of their loyalty and commitment to a man whom God had ordained as arrowhead leadership. The days are coming when we will love each other in purity as Jonathan did David. These days I am seeing the grace of an apostolic father breaking out with an integrity of relationship among my sons and daughters. This is giving me the power to negotiate the destiny of nations and not be ashamed as I stand before satanic strongholds and before my enemies at the gate of cities God has given to me as an inheritance.

Psalms 127:4-5
"Like arrows in the hand of a warrior, so are the children of one's youth. How blessed is the man whose quiver is full of them; they will not be ashamed When they speak with their enemies in the gate."

Moved Without Compromise To Deliver The Unadulterated Truth Of God

The breakthrough believers continued to teach and preach what they heard from the apostles in Jerusalem. The persecution had separated them physically but they did not compromise on what they had received as truth and doctrine from the apostles. Though they were not directly under the presence of any delegated authority and leadership, these believers obeyed the strong convictions of their hearts. They were practising believers rather than just being hearers of the word!

They delivered what they received without adulterating or compromising the message of truth. Often the truth taught is diluted through the lives of those who represent us in leadership and thus an incomplete truth is delivered to the next generation.

The truth that is not modelled by the hearers has lost the grace of impartation and implementation. When the truth is lived out before it is delivered, the spirit life of truth is made flesh and we will receive grace upon grace.

John 1:14
"And the Word became flesh, and dwelt among us, and we saw His glory, glory as of the only begotten from the Father, full of grace and truth."

John 1:16
"For of His fullness we have all received, and grace upon grace."

When the truth is lived and becomes flesh in our lives, it is not just truth taught but also grace given for obedience and implementation. People will receive special grace as they listen to the truth we are imparting. They will be able to go out and do it. They will find the ability to practice and apply what they are hearing from us.

> Acts 20:32
> *""And now I commend you to God and to the word of His grace, which is able to build you up and to give you the inheritance among all those who are sanctified.""*

> Acts 20:20
> *"......how I did not shrink from declaring to you anything that was profitable, and teaching you publicly and from house to house......."*

> Acts 20:27
> *""For I did not shrink from declaring to you the whole purpose of God.""*

As pastors we need to develop a way of continually checking with our leadership whether they are living the standards of truth taught to them. If not, they could contaminate the flow and perception of the unadulterated truth into the next generation. We don't want the next generation to receive "genetically modified spiritual food" because the investment and hope we are building towards the future will come crashing down. Breakthrough believers are trustworthy and they will live out the truth and deliver it as they have received of the Lord *(1 Corinthians 11:23)*.

Moved In Progressive Revelation To Stay Relevant

Breakthrough believers have the ability to move in progressive revelations in order to bring fresh update in present truth to keep the church relevant in the now. The apostles in Jerusalem upon hearing that God was moving in Samaria (half Jews) sent Peter and John to provide apostolic input into the region *(Acts 8:14,25)*. God also used Paul to reach the Hellenistic Jews *(Acts 9:29)* and Peter to reach the household of Cornelius *(Acts 10)* so that news of Gentiles receiving the Word of God spread everywhere *(Acts 11:1)*.

Believers who came by divine guidance to Antioch moved in the Spirit and started to reach out to the Greeks and the Gentile community there *(Acts 11:20-21)*. The hand of the Lord Jesus came mighty upon them and many who believed turned to the Lord. This company of breakthrough believers was led by the same Spirit that was leading the apostles to reach outside the Jewish community. They followed the Holy Spirit and tapped into the same flow as the apostles. There were no email updates or internet links to plot out the current move of the Holy Spirit. They were so pliable to the Holy Spirit that the same Spirit that was leading the apostles in Jerusalem was also leading the breakthrough believers in another geographic locality.

This distinctive quality of the breakthrough believers is the ingredient that allowed the revival of the Holy Spirit to spread quickly across the Roman Empire. They became very perceptive to the progressive revelation; not just to the fresh moves of the Holy Spirit, but also the restoration of truths.

Blessed is the pastor who has believers in his church who are attentively listening to God's voice in their daily lives. They will be a tremendous encouragement to the pastor who is hearing from God. They will help establish what God is saying through the pastor by their own testimony and sensitivity in the Holy Spirit. They will help consolidate the experiences at the grassroots in the church because they are able to hear and confirm the directions of the man of God.

> Luke 24:33-35
> *"And they got up that very hour and returned to Jerusalem, and found gathered together the eleven and those who were with them, saying, "The Lord has really risen and has appeared to Simon." They began to relate their experiences on the road and how He was recognized by them in the breaking of the bread."*

It creates a meaningful sense of destiny among the people. The sheep are hearing the voice of the shepherd and all the lambs follow as they observe the sheep following the shepherd without any conflict or inner struggles. It can be very frustrating for a pastor to see a non-responsive congregation when he delivers his message placed upon his heart by God.

Breakthrough believers are able to hear, identify and wholly respond to God's voice as it flows through His leadership.

> Proverbs 20:12
> *"The hearing ear and the seeing eye, The LORD has made both of them."*

Every breakthrough believer must be trained to move progressively in present truth so that they can set the standards of His Word for the people following them. These present truths bring us into the relevance of today's move and establish us as choice instruments to propagate it to the next generation.

Moved Under Subjection To Spiritual Authority

Breakthrough believers have the ability to move under subjection to spiritual authority breaking the spirit of rebellion and witchcraft while restoring the honour for spiritual leadership function. This company of believers have learned what it means to subject and submit themselves to God and divine authority.

They have first submitted themselves to the hand of God and now they are submitting themselves to Barnabas who was the sent one from Jerusalem. Though it was the believers who pioneered the church in Antioch, yet they subjected it to the leadership of the apostolic man.

Acts 11:21-22

"And the hand of the Lord was with them, and a large number who believed turned to the Lord. The news about them reached the ears of the church at Jerusalem, and they sent Barnabas off to Antioch."

Acts 11:26

"and when he had found him, he brought him to Antioch. And for an entire year they met with the church and taught considerable numbers; and the disciples were first called Christians in Antioch."

All who dwell within the House must be willing to put themselves under spiritual authority. An ability to yield to God's appointed and delegated leadership speaks of being submissive and teachable. The believers in Antioch set the apostolic pattern for churches in the future. When God assigns apostolic men to the places where God's move had already begun, the local company of believers must learn to yield to these "sent men" so that God can take the church further through them.

This happened with Peter and John, as they walked into a revived city of Samaria. Philip had gone into Samaria and started the work with the demonstration of the Holy Spirit. When the apostles came, Philip yielded to the apostles' input and foundation laying of the church in Samaria. He allowed the apostles to speak into the lives of those under his care. The apostles provided apostolic impartation by the laying on of hands. The deep rooted problems and seeds of the enemy were rooted out and a new foundation was built for the future *(Acts 8:20-24)*.

We need to build a clear paradigm concerning covering and authority into the minds of breakthrough believers. When they operate under covering and under authority, breakthrough believers can become instruments to destroy strongholds and witchcraft. The spirit of lawlessness will not dwell within the church. Men will not set up their own line of authority and walk in rebellion.

This ability to walk under total subjection to divine and spiritual authority will

provide a pattern for the new generation of believers to rise in our midst. They can bring the honour of leadership and government back into the church. All "spiritual authority" stems out of the Senior Pastor in the local church. Every leader who walks in honour and in submission to him in wholesome relationship can exercise spiritual authority.

Their "delegated authority" is a specific measure of authority within their sphere of responsibility and role function. When they are under spiritual authority, operating under delegated authority, they represent the man from whom they have received their commissioning to function in their leadership role.

Alternatively, men can use their delegated authority and function within the church without being under covering, in so doing they break their honour and loyalty to the one that is their primary source of life and authority in the local church. Some men who have strong giftings, talents and calling do not feel the need to have anyone over them because of the strong "functional authority" they carry in exercising their ministry. These men pose a danger to those whom they are ministering to because they are not under the spirit authority and covering.

When the prodigal son returned, the father told the servants to bring out the best robe and place it upon him. The best robe was not a new robe. The best robe was the robe the master of the function or ceremony uses. It represents the head of the feast. It represents the host and the highest authority in the gathering. The father covered the son with his robes. The covering protected him from being exposed and becoming vulnerable to attacks.

The word "covering" is often associated with those who have authority over you. However, the beauty of covering is not about the authority over us but rather the protection over us. The word is used to imply a shade under which the grapes grow. It is a protecting hedge or fence or shade that allows other plants to grow under. The tender plants are not to be grown in open direct heat of the sunlight. They are to be protected by the shade of other plants that can take the heat and sunlight.

Those plants take the intensity of the heat while protecting the young plants from being destroyed. Those who are our covering take the bullets for us. They are attacked first because they are the hedge around our lives. They allow us to grow to our full potential while they face the onslaughts of the enemy. We grow at their expense. They cover us in prayer, with their counsel, with their expertise and with their faith. They are raised by God over our lives to guard us until we come to maturity. The wickedness of the devil does not touch us first as the covering shade is our first line of defence. The enemy cannot come in to destroy as our covering and oversight provide the wall of protection for our lives.

Who is your covering? Who is the line of defence for you? Who is taking the bullets for you in your journey towards maturity? Who covers you in prayer and guards you in counsel? Who is the one who has said to the resident innkeeper to charge all your expenses to his account? That is your covering!

> Luke 10:35
> *"On the next day he took out two denarii and gave them to the innkeeper and said, "Take care of him; and whatever more you spend, when I return I will repay you.""*

We need someone in our lives who will mentor and father us; someone who will stand alongside us until we have come into our full potential and calling in God. We need this covering, shade and hedge of protection. We need someone who is magnanimous; who will stand by us believing in us as God believes in us. Barnabas could see the grace of God on the breakthrough believers and he encouraged them with resolute heart to remain true to the Lord.

We will always rise higher if someone believes in us and motivates us to reach for the highest. A covering will do more than just believe in us, they will carry us there. How desperately we need these bighearted fathers in the church today. Most mentors we trusted ended up being our tormentors!

Coming under authority is a powerful concept that can revolutionise everything that happens in the apostolic church. When we come under the authority of a person, we can then operate in the measure of his authority and represent that authority. When a General summons five privates to accompany him to a restricted building, they have access into the building on the grounds of the General's stature and authority. They walk into that building covered by

his authority and thus have access into what he has access to. When we are in Christ we can operate in the authority we do not possess on our own as individuals. We can operate in His authority and in His stature.

> Luke 10:19-20
> *"Behold, I have given you authority to tread on serpents and scorpions, and over all the power of the enemy, and nothing will injure you. Nevertheless do not rejoice in this, that the spirits are subject to you, but rejoice that your names are recorded in heaven."*

The literal sense of *verse 20* reads as follows:

> *"... that the spirits are subject to you as individuals but rejoice greatly that your names are intertwined and weaved together as one certified in the heavenlies."*

Our names are bound together with Christ and authenticated and authorised to function with legality and validity! If we understand that the power of coming under authority is to operate under the authority of the one we are representing, we will joyfully come under submission. Often the teachings on authority are used to bring obedience among a company of rebellious, unwilling people. It will backfire. We cannot expect those who do not have within them the seal of God's government to come into submission to God's appointed delegated authority in the church. Those who fail the test of submitting to the government of the kingdom will have their rebellious natures revealed under these authority structures!

Moved Collectively And Corporately Towards Destiny

Breakthrough believers have the ability to move collectively and corporately as a church by true commitment and loyalty to leadership towards the common destiny assigned to us by God. Most believers act as individuals with a personal agenda in life who are only in church to fulfil their religious obligations of Sunday services.

Most believers who have not been renewed in their thinking by kingdom paradigms use the church to nourish and strengthen themselves so that they can perform well in the world systems. "I am all prayed up, fired up and spiritually equipped so that I can do well as a believer in my job, school and business."

This prevailing mindset causes them to prioritise the activities in the world and their remaining time to be left for the church and its activities. To live for the kingdom is still a foreign thought and concept to a majority of believers.

> Matthew 6:33
> *"But seek first His kingdom and His righteousness, and all these things will be added to you."*

The kingdom we are told to seek is not outside or in the heavens coming down but inside of us. When God's governance is properly established within our hearts, minds, emotions and lifestyle, there will be righteousness, peace and joy in the Holy Ghost *(Romans 14:17).*

The kingdom principles of *Matthew 5, 6* and *7* allows the kingdom government to become evident in the life of breakthrough believers. These principles are life principles that build the core values into us. These core values must be within us before church activities or role functions are placed or added to us.

The kingdom must be established within us by allowing the government of God to manifest itself in our daily living. When everything that is not of the kingdom is shaken and removed from our lives, we have a kingdom that cannot be shaken.

> Hebrews 12:27-28
> *"This expression, 'Yet once more,' denotes the removing of those things which can be shaken, as of created things, so that those things which cannot be shaken may remain. Therefore, since we receive a kingdom which cannot be shaken, let us show gratitude, by which we may offer to God an acceptable service with reverence and awe......"*

God can add to our lives all these things which the Gentile seek, only when the kingdom government is established in us. The things of this world can easily corrupt, contaminate and destroy our lives if God's nature is not in our lives. Without first partaking His nature and coming under His rule, all these things the heathen seek can wipe us out in destruction. Most of us are not under kingdom rule and governance so to handle wealth, riches, fame, fortune or success. We have to be bigger than success if we are to handle our success well. We must have kingdom government firmly established in our hearts if we are to go in to plunder the devil's goods. It is because of this lack of kingdom rule and governance that believers become so preoccupied in the world system and only come to church at their convenience. The church is to them a place of last resort, when all else fail they turn to God!

Breakthrough believers have kingdom government in their lives and they make it their priority to be in the Father's house to further the Father's purposes here on the earth. Only those who are growing in wisdom and stature and in favour with God and men, will know the power of total involvement in the Father's house *(Luke 2:49,52)*.

Those who have served for the furtherance of God's government in their own lives will choose corporate lifestyles within the House. The book of *Acts* gives us evidence of a breakthrough company who sold their property and possessions and shared with all who were in need. This company devoted themselves to corporate living and community expression. They were knitted together, built and framed through fellowship, breaking of bread, prayer and the apostles' teaching. They carried the spirit of sacrifice and were bound together to pursue purpose and destiny. They stood together in the midst of persecution and prayed through for God's deliverance as they committed themselves afresh to God's commission.

Acts 4:29-32

"'And now, Lord, take note of their threats, and grant that Your bond-servants may speak Your word with all confidence, while You extend Your hand to heal, and signs and wonders take place through the name of Your holy servant Jesus.' And when they had prayed, the place where they had gathered together was shaken,

and they were all filled with the Holy Spirit and began to speak the word of God with boldness. And the congregation of those who believed were of one heart and soul; and not one of them claimed that anything belonging to him was his own, but all things were common property to them."

Moved With A Prevailing Mentality To Influence The Community

They had the ability to move with a prevailing mentality to impact the community and influence the society. Breakthrough believers make things happen so that their impact will ripple into the society. They create an impact on those around them by what they do and who they are. When the breakthrough believers in the book of *Acts* broke the race and the cultural barrier, the hand of God moved sovereignly and many who believed turned to the Lord.

This is a very interesting account because most believers today still have their eyes and focus set on the things of the world. Those who believe must turn their faces to the One their heart is seeking. In so many church believers' hearts are set upon the cares of this world and the deceitfulness of riches. Though they have turned to God, their hearts are still wandering in the affairs of this world.

2 Timothy 2:4
"No soldier in active service entangles himself in the affairs of everyday life, so that he may please the one who enlisted him as a soldier."

When Barnabas came to Antioch, he took the breakthrough believers to a new level and a considerable number were brought to the Lord. These believers were set in their hearts to create an impact on their society. Barnabas left for Tarsus and brought Saul into the leadership of that church. Together they taught the church an entire year and saw a substantial growth in the church.

Now the community was taking notice at what was happening. They were seeing the difference this company of believers were making in the city of Antioch. The believers were acting and living like Christ. The community was greatly impacted by this manifestation of Christ's life and likeness that they called them Christians; meaning "Christ ones". The community was able to identify a new breed that resembled the Christ. They became aware of Christ and the gospel by observing the lives of these believers.

We can see in *Acts 11:27-30*, that the church at Antioch also became involved in touching the community of believers in Judea. This was beyond their locality yet their influence was felt in the churches in Judea. Their involvement in mission giving became a very powerful testimony of God's deep work in their hearts and lives.

Breakthrough believers are not only able to affect those in their community but their testimony will begin to influence others everywhere. They will become a model of a New Testament church that is influencing the region. The churches in Rome and Thessalonica were also powerful testimonies of churches that were affecting the faith of the believers in the entire region.

> Romans 1:8
> *"First, I thank my God through Jesus Christ for you all, because your faith is being proclaimed throughout the whole world."*
>
> 1 Thessalonians 1:6-8
> *"You also became imitators of us and of the Lord, having received the word in much tribulation with the joy of the Holy Spirit, so that you became an example to all the believers in Macedonia and in Achaia. For the word of the Lord has sounded forth from you, not only in Macedonia and Achaia, but also in every place your faith toward God has gone forth, so that we have no need to say anything."*

Author's Note:

To complete this series on the characteristics of breakthrough believers please read Chapters 22 to 25 of *"Apostolic Strategies Affecting Nations."*

Chapters 22 and 23 deal with the four types of believers in the church. This is a very important part of our study on Breakthrough Believer as it allows the Pastor to discover the types of people he has and how to raise the right kind of people. It also helps the Pastors to deal with the resistors effectively. The apostolic wisdom required in this people management process is revealed in these pages.

Chapter 24 deals with the breakthrough believers moving under spiritual authority. The concepts of spiritual authority are dealt in detail. This chapter allows the reader to know what it means to walk in spiritual authority.

Chapter 25 deals with breakthrough believers moving in the Anointing. This is an amazing chapter that causes us to see that there are two types of anointing that graces a believer; one equips his life and the other empowers his ministry. We can discover how his life forms the foundational basis for effective ministry in the Holy Spirit. Many have learned to work with the anointing but not with the Anointed One.

Be Blessed!

Chapter Eight

WINNING MENTALITY OF BREAKTHROUGH BELIEVERS

In this chapter we are dealing with the prevailing mindset of breakthrough believers. It is this paradigm and thinking pattern that frees the believer to act in the way he should.

> Proverbs 23:7(a)
> *"For as he thinks within himself, so he is......"*

The quality of our mentality often affects our perspectives and decisions. It drastically affects our attitudes or the way we choose to do things.

"The last of the human freedoms is to choose one's attitude in any given set of circumstances."

– [Victor Frankl *-survivor of a Nazi concentration camp-*]

The prevailing thinking pattern within a breakthrough believer fashions his behaviour patterns. This prevailing thinking pattern allows the Holy Spirit's insights to be received effectively. The mind that is set on the Spirit is life and peace. It is not hostile against God.

Romans 8:6-7

"For the mind set on the flesh is death, but the mind set on the Spirit is life and peace, because the mind set on the flesh is hostile toward God; for it does not subject itself to the law of God, for it is not even able to do so"

It is yielded to the working of the Holy Spirit, it is able to establish accurate patterns of behaviour, and it is well pleasing before God. This renewed thinking pattern forms an excellent attitude for kingdom living.

Philippians 2:5

"Have this attitude in yourselves which was also in Christ Jesus,..."

Breakthrough believers have a winning mentality that spreads over seven areas of their lifestyle. This renewed thinking pattern allows these seven areas to become strong foundations for wholesome character and righteous expression in a believer.

The Area Of Witness

The first area of their winning mentality is in the area of witness. The breakthrough believer is a witness of all that he has seen and heard on a first hand experience in his encounter with God.

1 John 1:1-3

"What was from the beginning, what we have heard, what we have seen with our eyes, what we have looked at and touched with our hands, concerning the Word of Life and the life was manifested, and we have seen and testify and proclaim to you the eternal life, which was with the Father and was manifested to us what we have seen and heard we proclaim to you also, so that you too may have fellowship with us; and indeed our fellowship is with the Father, and with His Son Jesus Christ."

He has handled the word of life and has experienced the eternal life here on this earth. He is seeing the invisible, heavenly dimension manifesting in the visible earthly life. He is touching the eternal life and dimensions by touching, hearing, seeing and knowing the Word of life.

> John 6:68
> *"Simon Peter answered Him, "Lord, to whom shall we go? You have words of eternal life.""*

Jesus was the Word of eternal life. He provided access to eternity. By touching and partaking Jesus the Word, we can enter into the eternal life and partake divine nature.

> John 1:1-3
> *"In the beginning was the Word, and the Word was with God, and the Word was God. He was in the beginning with God. All things came into being through Him, and apart from Him nothing came into being that has come into being."*

All things that have come into the visible realm from the invisible have come through Jesus. In the Word was life. This life was with the Father. This life is the light of men and when men walk in this light, they will not stumble or be destroyed by darkness.

A witness is one who has seen and heard what had happened. He was there when the incident occurred. His being there and experiencing it firsthand, gives him the power to testify. His testimony carries weight and his affirmation is true.

> Proverbs 14:24(a)
> *"The crown of the wise is their riches,......"*

The firsthand testimony of a witness saves lives in the court of law. It defends the innocent and judges those who are wrong. A breakthrough believer's personal encounter with God gives him the authority to touch and impact lives. He presses into God so that he may know the truth and the revelations of the

Spirit. He desires to live these truths out so that he may impart it to others. We have to choose to learn more accurately if we want to impart into others.

> 2 Timothy 2:2
> *"The things which you have heard from me in the presence of many witnesses, entrust these to faithful men who will be able to teach others also."*

God is raising these believers to become forerunners and first-fruits so that they can experience and know the activities of the Holy Spirit. They can then model it in their own lives so that others can live and be blessed by their life and sacrifice.

> 2 Corinthians 4:11-12
> *"For we who live are constantly being delivered over to death for Jesus' sake, so that the life of Jesus also may be manifested in our mortal flesh. So death works in us, but life in you."*

The winning mentality of a breakthrough believer is established on this area of witness so that others can find the way of hope and God encounter.

> 1 John 1:3
> *"......what we have seen and heard we proclaim to you also, so that you too may have fellowship with us; and indeed our fellowship is with the Father, and with His Son Jesus Christ."*

By fellowshipping with breakthrough believers, we can come into a deeper encounter with the Father and the Lord Jesus Christ. They become the choice instruments for God to penetrate the region and impact the lives of the people around them.

The Area Of Worship

The second area of their winning mentality is in the area of worship. Breakthrough believers are true worshippers who worship the Father in spirit and truth. Worship is not centred around an activity but around "hearts reaching out to His throne."

A breakthrough believer knows that God is WORTHY. His "WORTHSHIP" is without question the supreme thought in their minds. God does not just deserve our praise, He is worthy of praise. A breakthrough believer gives to God the highest honour in worship.

He uses his heart and mouth to bring forth praises. God is enthroned upon the praises of his lips. His worship builds a throne for God who is invisible to come into the visible realm and manifest His power and glory.

> Psalms 22:3
> *"Yet You are holy, O You who are enthroned upon the praises of Israel."*

Their attitude of worship is formed by acknowledging the truth that Jesus is always worthy despite what they feel or think. We are created to worship and not participating in worship only reveals the lack of kingdom purpose. We know that the Father seeks true worshippers who will fulfil His requirements for worship in spirit and truth. There are many who bring an unacceptable worship like Cain who chose his own standards of presentations to God in worship. But we are very convinced that the body and all its expressions of love and adoration must accompany the true spirit of worship.

> Romans 12:1
> *"Therefore I urge you, brethren, by the mercies of God, to present your bodies a living and holy sacrifice, acceptable to God, which is your spiritual service of worship."*

Mental attitude and maturity are needed as we think of ways to honour Him. All our worship expressions must embrace our emotions for worship to mean something deeper than mere words. Our expression of worship is reflected in our face, carried in our voice and demonstrated in and through our body. The expressions of pure worship must be enhanced by our emotions, sustained by our passion and motivated by our thoughts of honour and worthiness.

A breakthrough believer's mind is centred on giving worship that is due to His name. They do not just perform worship but carry a spirit of worship. The spirit of worship refers to the life and heart of a believer and his ability to pour out his heart in intense passion of adoration and worship. The spirit of worship causes a believer to yield to the Holy Spirit to learn of new ways of expressions of worship that are pleasing before God. The spirit of worship is formed in a believer as he presents his lifestyle of devotion, being hungry and thirsty for God's Presence. The believer's winning mentality in this area of worship keeps his heart continually pliable and yielded to the Holy Spirit. He is acutely sensitive to God's indwelling presence within himself and walks in a God-consciousness that keeps him free from sin and unrighteousness.

The Area Of Work

The third area of the winning mentality of breakthrough believers is in the area of work. Breakthrough believers have a positive attitude towards work. Most people are allergic to work. Some work hard while others hardly work.

> John 4:34
> *"Jesus said to them, "My food is to do the will of Him who sent Me and to accomplish His work.""*

These believers are fruitful, functioning members. The act of doing His Will brings nourishment to our souls. It will cause the life of God to enable and refresh us. It will quicken our hearts with a greater desire to please Him more as we yield our will to do His will. When this prevailing mentality rules over

our thinking patterns, we initiate a sovereign move in the Spirit over our lives. When we do His will by yielding our will, a work is accomplished by God in the spirit realm.

By obeying His will, for example, to give to a particular financial need, a work is done permanently in our hearts and minds. Maybe our secret fears of future lack or the memories of the past sufferings due to lack will be dealt with in our lives. By choosing to do His will, we release God to do a work in us through the circumstance. His purpose for asking us to do what we were told to do will be done. When we do His will, a sovereign work is established in the Spirit realm. When God's work is accomplished, the harvest is released upon our lives.

> John 4:35
> *"'Do you not say, "There are yet four months, and then comes the harvest?" Behold, I say to you, lift up your eyes and look on the fields, that they are white for harvest.'"*

The harvest is brought forward four months ahead of the normal pattern and schedule. There is a quickening grace and acceleration in the Spirit to bring our harvest to us. Whenever God wants us to do His will and obey His word, He is seeking an opportunity to complete a work in us and through us in the Spirit. Then He will send us the harvest. The future harvest rushes towards us. We do not have to run into the future to look for our harvest and reward. The harvest and the future reward is running towards us.

This mental attitude towards work and doing His will propels the breakthrough believers into the pathway of acceleration. This attitude causes the believers to progress and mature quickly.

There is another aspect of work that motivates breakthrough believers and it's the work of building the apostolic base. They are consumed with zeal for building the church. If we study the book of Nehemiah, we can see that the zeal of God's people allowed them to rise above every turmoil and limitation to build the walls in Jerusalem. Their prevailing mindset positioned them to thrive in the midst of chaos. They built an impregnable work in the midst of their enemies.

Nehemiah 4:1-5

"Now it came about that when Sanballat heard that we were rebuilding the wall, he became furious and very angry and mocked the Jews. He spoke in the presence of his brothers and the wealthy men of Samaria and said, 'What are these feeble Jews doing? Are they going to restore it for themselves? Can they offer sacrifices? Can they finish in a day? Can they revive the stones from the dusty rubble even the burned ones?' Now Tobiah the Ammonite was near him and he said, 'Even what they are building--if a fox should jump on it, he would break their stone wall down!' Hear, O our God, how we are despised! Return their reproach on their own heads and give them up for plunder in a land of captivity. Do not forgive their iniquity and let not their sin be blotted out before You, for they have demoralized the builders."

A quick look at *Nehemiah* reveals that they PROTECTED THE WORK from the effects of money and religious politics. They did not allow the wealthy men of Samaria (half-Jews) to gain control over their destiny. Their intimidation and fear-mongering could not destroy the zeal of God's people.

Nehemiah and the builders had a MIND TO WORK.

Nehemiah 4:6

"So we built the wall and the whole wall was joined together to half its height, for the people had a mind to work."

They refused to allow the enemy to stop the work that God had begun through them in Judah. They prayed, kept vigilant and INSPIRED THE WORKERS so that their spirits would be refreshed and energized.

Nehemiah 4:9

"But we prayed to our God, and because of them we set up a guard against them day and night."

Intimidation can demoralize our spirits but keeping a strong prayer life in the Spirit can cause us to become buoyant in rough and turbulent waters. The enemies of Judah PLANNED TO STOP THE WORK, but the prophetic anointing exposed the schemes of the enemy to these builders. The attitude of not yielding to the schemes of the enemy became a barricade and a strong fortress against the wicked men who tried to exploit the fears of the people of God.

> Nehemiah 4:11-12, 15
> *"Our enemies said, 'They will not know or see until we come among them, kill them and put a stop to the work.' When the Jews who lived near them came and told us ten times, 'They will come up against us from every place where you may turn,' ... When our enemies heard that it was known to us, and that God had frustrated their plan, then all of us returned to the wall, each one to his work."*

Nehemiah stationed each man in his accurate place and positioned them so that EACH ONE CAN BE EFFECTIVE IN HIS WORK. He taught them to be very effective as builders as well as soldiers, and trained them to carry their load with ONE HAND DOING THE WORK AND THE OTHER HOLDING A WEAPON.

> Nehemiah 4:17
> *"Those who were rebuilding the wall and those who carried burdens took their load with one hand doing the work and the other holding a weapon."*

Breakthrough believers must be trained to become multi-pronged so that they are effective with both left hand and right hand. Nehemiah was a strategist and as THE WORK BECAME EXTENSIVE, he devised a way to keep the work guarded and caused people to rally to him at the sound of the trumpet.

> Nehemiah 4:19-20
> *"I said to the nobles, the officials and the rest of the people, "The work is great and extensive, and we are separated on the wall far from one another. "At whatever place you hear the sound of the trumpet, rally to us there. Our God will fight for us.""*

The prophetic voice must cause every believer in the church to rally together behind the arrowhead leadership so that everyone is working towards the

common purpose and destiny God has assigned for us. This mental attitude towards God's work will propel breakthrough believers "to occupy till He comes" *(Luke 19:13)*.

The Area Of War

The fourth area of the winning mentality of breakthrough believers is in the area of war. Breakthrough believers possess a mentality for war. They have a fighting spirit, and are often spoiling for adventure! We are called to fight the good fight of faith *(2 Timothy 4:7)*.

If we do not fight our battles, we cannot wear the crown. A lot of church believers are carried in the arms of others and many others fight their battles for them. They remain inexperienced and immature as their pastors fight on their behalf. God wants us to train our hands for war. He wants us to be able to slay our enemies so that we will know what it means to be a victor and an overcomer rather than be a victim.

A breakthrough believer's mentality is poised to fight his own battles. He is ready to take the challenge to pursue his enemies until he overtakes them and recovers all that has been stolen from him.

> 1 Samuel 30:8
> *"David inquired of the LORD, saying, 'Shall I pursue this band? Shall I overtake them?' And He said to him, 'Pursue, for you will surely overtake them, and you will surely rescue all.'"*

Every breakthrough believer must be taught to become a champion by rising in the power of the Holy Spirit to overcome every sin and personal inadequacy and limitation. The mentality and attitude not to be intimidated is very essential in becoming a champion. The enemy will often try to demoralize us so that we will give up on the challenge. There are six aspects of intimidation we will discover in *Nehemiah 4:2* which often push the believer to quit or abort his pursuit towards total victory.

Intimidation is the act of continual harassment until the person's wall of resistance is broken down and he starts to belittle and despise what he is and what he has. It can latch onto a person until it demoralizes him.

Nehemiah 4:2
"He spoke in the presence of his brothers and the wealthy men of Samaria and said, 'What are these feeble Jews doing? Are they going to restore it for themselves? Can they offer sacrifices? Can they finish in a day? Can they revive the stones from the dusty rubble even the burned ones?'"

A. Intimidation Will Attack Our Character

The first area intimidation will attack us in, is in our "character."

"What are these feeble Jews doing?"

Nehemiah is not feeble, he is noble. The enemies' accusation can harm the way we feel about ourselves. The enemy will tell us that we do not have what it takes to get the job done. We do not have the personality, the style or the church is too small and we'll never make it. This call is bigger than us and thus we should not embrace it or we will be put to shame. Moses was attacked by this spirit of intimidation. *"Who am I that I should go to Pharaoh?" (Exodus 3:11)*

Our identity andf who we are is established in discovering His identity and who He is. Our completeness is in being connected to him. "I Am who I Am" is the reply to the question of "who am I?"

Colossians 3:3-4
"For you have died and your life is hidden with Christ in God. When Christ, who is our life, is revealed, then you also will be revealed with Him in glory."

When Christ, who is our life, is revealed, we who are hidden in Him will

also be revealed. He must first be revealed, and then we will be revealed at the revelation of Christ Himself.

B. Intimidation Will Attack Our Motives

The second aspect of intimidation that can destroy us is the attack on our "motives."

"Are they going to restore it for themselves?"

They accuse us of wanting to be somebody, to be doing it for the money or for some hidden agenda.

The attack causes us to doubt our own integrity and forces us to question our motives. It forces us to feel guilty about something we are sure is not within our own hearts. The devil will try to confuse us between pride and boldness. The people who are sincere and want to serve God and do their best often become prey to intimidation.

C. Intimidation Will Attack Our Qualification

The third aspect of intimidation is the attacks on our "qualification".

"Can they offer sacrifices?"

They do not have the priestly qualifications to offer sacrifices. They do not have the authority, the titles and paper qualification to function in what they are doing.

Intimidation will attack the call of God on our lives. It is the call of God that sanctions the man to function. God will attest to our call with many signs, wonders and miracles. He will rise for our vindication and place His approval upon our lives. This lack of approval has derailed many ministries as they have sought after man's approval and the seat of honour among men *(Matthew 23:1-7)*.

D. Intimidation Will Attack Our Zeal

The fourth aspect of intimidation is the attack on our "zeal."

"Can they finish it in a day?"

The enemies will question our wisdom in trying to do so much within so short a time and with so little resources. They will attempt to pour cold water on our zeal by trying to question our passion. They will discourage us and warn us of burn-out and that we are ambitious to attempt these great things. We should not strive but learn to "rest" in God. We are admonished not to "push it in our own strength and produce it in the flesh." All these attacks are to destroy our passion which is the driving force that will help us finish the course set before our lives.

E. Intimidation Will Attack Our Grace

The fifth area in which intimidation attacks us is in our "anointing and grace."

"Can they revive the stones from the dusty rubble even the burnt ones?"

"Do they possess the anointing to revive the stones that have been burnt and bruised? Do they have the grace to turn these cities around?" They will force us to doubt our grace and our spiritual capacities. They will not recognize the grace on our lives which equips us for the task we have been called to do. Do not allow others to despise the grace God has given to us.

It is unique and it is God's pleasure to equip us in that manner. Barnabas witnessed the grace of God in operation in the lives of the believers in Antioch, and he encouraged them with resolute heart to remain true to God.

F. Intimidation Will Attack Our Hope

The last area intimidation will attack usin, is in our "hope for a better future."

"Even what they are building – if a fox should jump on it, he would break their stone wall down!"

Foxes trot carefully when they are walking on a wall. A fox is a sure footed animal being light in its steps. They predicted that even with minimum efforts and weight the walls are doomed to collapse. They mocked them that their utmost effort was useless and unprofitable. They despised their work of building, saying that a simple act can cause a great disaster on the wall. They were despised because the enemy believed whatever they were building had no future and will be in ruins. They believed there can be no future protection or hope for the people of Judah and whatever they were building will be in utter ruins.

We can see from all these aspects that intimidation can build serious inroads into our emotions and thinking patterns and demoralize the builders from building. God is raising breakthrough believers to walk with a prevailing mindset so that they will rise to the challenge and intimidate the intimidators. We are to rise boldly like lions to frighten fear out of the camp.

The Area Of Welfare

The fifth area of the winning mentality of breakthrough believers is in the area of "welfare." Their support for one another and the sense of brotherly responsibility is strongly etched into their thinking patterns. These believers provide strong emotional support by becoming their brothers' keepers giving one another preference *(Genesis 4:9)*. The reason why Cain asked whether he was his brother's keeper was because he was his brother's murderer!

Apostolic churches raise breakthrough believers who are able to connect with

one another on the basis of covenant. These believers were pressured from all angles in the book of *Acts* with persecution and death. They needed to stand with one another and strengthen each other. The apostles developed conducive cultures for such integration to take place. The apostles provided the needed dynamics and structures so that the people lived not as individuals, but as a kingdom community. The concepts of body life and corporate lifestyle ironed out personality differences and contention within the house.

The first miracle recorded after the day of Pentecost in *Acts 3* was a miracle that happened through team effort of Peter and John! Subsequently, they faced trials and persecution together as one man. The rulers and the elders who were gathered together for the inquiry, observed the confidence of Peter and John; they recognised them as having been with Jesus *(Acts 4:13).* The three fold cord cannot be broken.

When they were released they went to their own companions *(Acts 4:23)*. The network of covenant relationships within the kingdom community gave them renewed strength and continual access into the presence of God to further His purposes and will on the earth. They were able to synergize together and inspire each other to continue during the most turbulent times. Believers today need such a strong people connection within the house that will supply to their every need, not just financial, but spiritual and emotional as well.

> Acts 4: 31-33
> *"And when they had prayed, the place where they had gathered together was shaken, and they were all filled with the Holy Spirit and began to speak the word of God with boldness. And the congregation of those who believed were of one heart and soul; and not one of them claimed that anything belonging to him was his own, but all things were common property to them. And with great power the apostles were giving testimony to the resurrection of the Lord Jesus, and abundant grace was upon them all."*

The apostolic culture in the book of *Acts* was conducive for kingdom community integration and expression. We can create a synergized environment that will energize the people and become a catalyst for fresh moves of the Spirit. The

apostolic church must build this conducive atmosphere and culture to grow breakthrough believers.

The Area Of Worth

The sixth area of the winning mentality of breakthrough believers is in the area of worth. Breakthrough believers understand that they are created in the image and likeness of Jesus the Pattern Son. Our spirit has been recreated in His image. We are not the Son and the Son is not us. We are two different distinctive persons. We are modelled and recreated in our spirit in His image and likeness. In short, we have the same nature and characteristics in our spirits that at full maturity we will look and act like Him. Any confusion at this point will cause believers to walk in doctrinal error.

God raises the apostolic and prophetic ministry to build this foundation of Christ's life, nature and likeness into our spirit. These ministries have been given the awesome task to form the Christ within our spirit so that He is revealed in us.

"Jacob have I created, Israel have I formed" (Isaiah 43:1). We are a new creation but we need to be discipled and formed until Christ is seen in each of us.

> Galatians 4:19
> *"My children, with whom I am again in labor until Christ is formed in you........"*
>
> Ephesians 4:13
> *"......until we all attain to the unity of the faith, and of the knowledge of the Son of God, to a mature man, to the measure of the stature which belongs to the fullness of Christ."*

Potentially we have Christ's life and nature within our spirit. In fact, the Bible tells us that we have the Spirit of Christ in us. Our spirit has taken on the nature of the Spirit of Christ *(Romans 8:9)*.

Breakthrough believers are trained to live in the Spirit by allowing the Holy Spirit to dwell within us in full measure. When the Holy Spirit dwells within us, He has the freedom to fully express His life, thoughts and ways within our spirit, soul and body. When we are totally yielded to His sovereign control and come under His governance, we are living and walking in the Spirit *(Romans 8:9)*.

If this nature of Christ is in us or if the Spirit of Christ nature is in us, though our body is dead because it has experienced sin, yet our own spirit is alive because of righteousness. The body will decay because it has been conceived and brought forth with sin nature. Since the wages of sin is death, this body will eventually die, but our spirit having the nature of Christ is alive and active towards God. It is receiving fresh revelation from the Holy Spirit and is being renewed and refreshed every day *(2 Corinthians 4:16)*.

We are able to hear His Voice and commune with Him as our Father. When the Holy Spirit dwells within us, His "empowering" will bring us into a greater encounter with God. The Holy Spirit will lead us into all truth so that we are free in all our thinking patterns and become renewed in our minds *(John 16:13, Romans 12:2)*.

The Holy Spirit will cause us to become free from the spirit of slavery which will lead us to the fear of death *(Hebrews 2:15)*. This fear will keep us in subjection to all the elementary things of the world system and keep us in bondage. The Holy Spirit will lead us out of slavery into sonship by which we cry "Abba! Father!" *(Romans 8:15)*.

The Holy Spirit will quicken our mortal bodies which is destined to see death with the resurrection power that raised Jesus from the dead *(Romans 8:11)*. The Holy Spirit is releasing new life not only into our spirit, which is already alive because of righteousness, but also into our body so that instead of death working in us, resurrection power is working in us. As this resurrection life increases within our mortal body, our appointment with death will be further and further delayed. This will help increase our health and prolong our lives here on the earth.

There will be a generation of believers at the time of the Lord's second coming that would have defeated death because of the effectual working of the Holy Spirit's resurrection power in their mortal bodies.

All of creation is waiting for this day to break out on the sons of God as they were subject to futility not willingly but because of Him who subjected it in hope that one day all creation will be set free from its slavery to corruption in the freedom of the glory of the sons of God *(Romans 8:20-21)*.

God is raising a first-fruit company of the Spirit who will experience this redemption of the body and the full adoption as sons. There is no adoption as sons without the physical redemption of the body *(Romans 8:23)*. This is the reason why we are so integral to the consummation of the ages *(Hebrews 9:26,28)*. Creation waits for this final display of salvation for all mankind. Angels long to look into this divine drama of redemption.

The breakthrough believer's sense of worth is not in himself but in the purposes of God surrounding his life. He understands that he is not just an object of redemption but also the product of ultimate redemption. In his rising, the purposes of God will be fulfilled on the earth. The winning mentality of the breakthrough believer is established in the sense of true worth, being redeemed as sinners, but adopted as sons of the Most High; "but if sons, then heirs and fellow heirs with Christ" *(Romans 8:17)*.

In closing, let us see the mercy that God has shown us in Christ. God has not only chosen to save us from sin, but share all things with us through His Son Jesus.

> Ephesians 2:4-7
> *"But God, being rich in mercy, because of His great love with which He loved us, even when we were dead in our transgressions, made us alive together with Christ (by grace you have been saved), and raised us up with Him, and seated us with Him in the heavenly places in Christ Jesus, so that in the ages to come He might show the surpassing riches of His grace in kindness toward us in Christ Jesus."*

Hebrews 2:5-9

"For He did not subject to angels the world to come, concerning which we are speaking. But one has testified somewhere, saying, "WHAT IS MAN, THAT YOU REMEMBER HIM? OR THE SON OF MAN, THAT YOU ARE CONCERNED ABOUT HIM? YOU HAVE MADE HIM FOR A LITTLE WHILE LOWER THAN THE ANGELS; YOU HAVE CROWNED HIM WITH GLORY AND HONOR, AND HAVE APPOINTED HIM OVER THE WORKS OF YOUR HANDS; YOU HAVE PUT ALL THINGS IN SUBJECTION UNDER HIS FEET." For in subjecting all things to him, He left nothing that is not subject to him. But now we do not yet see all things subjected to him. But we do see Him who was made for a little while lower than the angels, namely, Jesus, because of the suffering of death crowned with glory and honor, so that by the grace of God He might taste death for everyone."

In reading the above verses, we can understand the integral part man plays in God's ultimate purpose which He carried out in Christ Jesus our Lord *(Ephesians 3:11)*.

We understand that it was man, not angels that were destined to rule. Though we have not seen the reality of this yet, we see Jesus who has become the forerunner of our future destiny. Jesus was made a little lower than the angels because of the suffering of death, but was crowned with glory and honour above all other. Now all things are being subjected to the Lord Jesus and all His enemies are becoming a footstool for His feet. In *Hebrews 2:8*, we are told of God's intention to subject all things to men whom He will redeem through His Son Jesus.

God will bring many sons to glory and honour. Jesus Himself will not be ashamed to call them His brethren, His flesh and His blood. It is to this company that angels are sent to tender service *(Hebrew 1:14)*. It is to this company that Jesus was sent to bring deliverance and help so that they can come into God's ultimate intention. God has chosen not to leave anything that will not be subject to men. Even death, sin, sickness and Satan will bow and be defeated by the redeemed man.

But NOW WE DO NOT YET SEE ALL THINGS SUBJECTED TO HIM BUT WE DO SEE JESUS! The "HIM" in this reference is not Jesus but the Corporate Man, the Body of Christ and the redeemed company of the first-fruits of the Holy Spirit here on the earth.

The breakthrough believers' winning mentality is deeply entrenched in their ultimate victory and destiny in Christ. They will be the crown and joy of the Lord Jesus. They will be the Bride of the Lamb forever.

The Area Of Wealth

The seventh area of the winning mentality of breakthrough believers is in the area of wealth. They are established in their understanding that they are not just givers of resources, but financiers of the kingdom. They live to be a source of supply for the work of God.

This mentality is different from those who just desire to be blessed for themselves and then apportion some money for the kingdom of God. These end time financiers know that God has called them to be positioned accurately in the world so that they can tap in the flow of finances and channel them into the kingdom. They know what it means to create interfaces into the systems of the world so that they are right where cash and wealth flows.

These men have the Kingdom of God and His righteousness positioned in their hearts. They have overcome the deceitfulness of riches and have risen above the love for money. They know that God has called them to plunder the house of the enemy and distribute his goods to those in the Kingdom of God.

God has shown that there is a new generation of "Josephs" rising in the earth today. They are being prepared by God to preserve the people of the kingdom in the future financial famine on the earth. There will be strains on the major economies of the earth. There will be financial crisis across the nations before a financial collapse of the monetary systems of the earth. God will raise up this company of Josephs to redistribute in apostolic power the wealth that remains.

They will save lives, properties and entire nations by the wisdom God will give to them. They are being selected and trained for the future. Study the life of Joseph as these men are already in the formation across the earth. They have been prepared for the future and for such a time as this. God will give them the "seven years of plenty and the seven years of famine." They will have wisdom to strategize with major corporations and whole governments in order to preserve and protect the people during those turbulent times of financial lack and crisis.

Joseph went through about fourteen years of major dealings before he came to the throne. His prophetic anointing was able to sustain him even in the prison as he interpreted the butler's and the baker's dreams. That Joseph generation is being prepared now for the future moments of glory. They are now learning to operate by divine principles. Let us look at some of these principles briefly as these principles fashion the thinking patterns of our breakthrough believers in these last days.

A. Moving From Ownership To Stewardship Mentality

The first principle is to move businessmen from the sense of ownership to an attitude of stewardship of God's resources. God is the owner of all things and the businessman is only a faithful steward. He must look after the businesses well with a spirit of excellence. He must be ready to release the resources to wherever it is needed and to where God directs it. He must never restrict God from reaching into his pocket and taking what He wants to distribute.

When we become God's pocket, He must be free to take out any amount He wants to give away. When a businessman thinks in terms of ownership he will control everything according to his mindset however, this mentality allows the businessman to transit from ownership to stewardship.

B. Giving For Advancement Not Maintenance Only

The second principle is to train businessmen and believers to give to where there is kingdom building, not just to needs. Mission giving must be re-evaluated as most giving has been because there is a need. These needs are endless and most times it is like a bottomless pit. Jesus said that the poor we will always have with us. We will need to do that which is needful.

Give where the kingdom of God is accurately positioned and built. Give to where there is consistent accurate building of the church. Those whom we support must reveal that what they are building is furthering the kingdom purpose for that region. There are needs everywhere and giving to just needs may not be accurately serving the purpose. We will have to study each situation and prioritize our giving.

C. Spiritual Positioning To Draw Wealth

The third principle is that the businessmen should be spiritually positioned to draw the wealth of the nations into the Kingdom of God, rather than use all their resources to compete with the world systems. Many businesses are using all their time, energy and resources to compete with the world's ever-changing systems. We need to keep our focus and faith on the favour and provision of the Lord. He will give us strategies and wisdom to move in His plans accurately. We do not have to copy from another, as God can give to us cutting edge products and strategies to make the difference. The pressure and the cares of the world can overwhelm us, making us feel like a grasshopper in the business world. God is raising a new breed with a spiritual position of stature to stand firm and not be shaken during the times of financial uncertainties.

D. Re-Structure And Re-Define To Be Relevant

The fourth principle that moves the kingdom businessman is that he needs to restructure and redefine his role functions and that of his business so that it is relevant to the time and environment they are operating in. Sometimes many in the business world carry huge titles with little job capabilities and capacities! Define the role before we assign the titles. Functions must be carried out in the spirit of excellence before titles and positions are set in concrete.

These end time financiers must be willing to re-adjust their thinking, restructure their operating systems and improve their customer service lines so that their businesses can break the bottleneck and propel growth.

E. Strategic Connections To The World Systems

The fifth principle is that the businessman must become a strategic connector in the world system so that he can become the channel for the redistribution of wealth and resources in the kingdom. It's about being in the right place at the right time and meeting the right people. Their people connectivity skills give them the leverage to perform better. The businessman must choose to believe that God will bring him before great men because of the grace and power He has given him.

> Proverbs 18:16
> *"A fool's lips bring strife, And his mouth calls for blows."*
>
> Deuteronomy 8:18
> *"'But you shall remember the LORD your God, for it is He who is giving you power to make wealth, that He may confirm His covenant which He swore to your fathers, as it is this day.'"*

F. A Mentality For Building The Church

The sixth principle for the businessman to become kingdom businessman is to develop the mentality of not just blessing the church but rather for the building of the church. The end time businessman financier does not give to every project and to every need. He prioritizes specific areas so that there can be systematic strategic building into the work.

Often the businessman's priority is for the retraining of the current leaders and the reproducing of a new generation. The greatest investment in the kingdom is not into bricks and mortar but into the lives of the people especially the leaders. We must give the best to the best of our people.

G. The Power To Make Wealth

Lastly, the kingdom businessman knows that God has given him power to make wealth because He wants to confirm His covenant with him. The businessman must now confirm his side of the covenant by living and using the power to make wealth for kingdom advancement. He will organise his finances so that he can be a greater source of supply. He must learn more effective ways in which to do business in order that he may have greater resources to participate with God in kingdom purposes.

He must become retrained and better equipped so that he may be at his best. He acquires wisdom, administrative skill and spirit anointing so that he can be at his best capacity to fulfil his part of the covenant keeping; to be God's supply line on the earth. God is raising a new breed of suppliers not just givers on the earth!

Chapter Nine

CHANGING BEHAVIOUR PATTERNS OF BREAKTHROUGH BELIEVERS

One of the most powerful ways to bring permanent change in people is to change their thinking patterns. The people's thinking patterns often attributes to why they act the way they do. We are not of the past, but our past thinking patterns program us to live a repeat of our past lifestyle. Every seed of the past which has been sown into our lives, programs us to relate to the present in the way it reads for us. The perspectives provided by these "seed thoughts" can keep us locked up in the past. We will keep repeating our fears and limitations as the past seed thoughts control us in a linear direction. Our present will be equal to our past and now our future is also becoming predictable because of the consequences of that which the past has made us to become.

> Proverbs 23:7
> *"For as he thinks within himself, so he is. ..."*

The condition of the woman with the issue of blood was getting worse and worse even though she was trying to use all the information and data she had. Her mind was programmed around what she knew and what she thought was best for her. She had come to a certain conclusion about herself and her needs. She had come to certain preferences she desired to have. She was saturated

with the past perspectives, preferences and prejudices!

Then she heard about Jesus *(Mark 5:27)*. It changed everything for her. What she heard penetrated deep into her mind and spirit. It caused a supernatural work that de-programmed her mind from many years of the past defeat, sickness and discouragement. It went deep into the recesses of her mind and de-programmed her mind from operating under the influence of the past information and thought patterns that kept her going in these cycles of defeat. It kept her turning to the same thing even though she was seeing no apparent results. She kept going to the same place even though her condition was getting worse.

The words she heard, gave her a new paradigm and thought pattern. It affected her thinking and gave her power to visualize the hope she saw in her mind. She was getting to see the miracle of her own healing in her mind. She understood the process and course of action she will have to take if what she is seeing in her mind (her vision, her dream) became a reality.

> Mark 5:28
> *"For she thought, 'If I just touch His garments, I will get well.'"*

She de-programmed herself from the influence of those old thoughts and re-programmed herself with the power of this new thought. It sets her free from the past. It helped her rise in the now and take the inspired action to see the miracle. She rose up in the spirit to take responsibility for her own miracle. She refused to let the twelve years of defeat and discouragement withhold her from receiving God's answer today. Today, was a new day. Today, was her day of salvation. Today, was the tomorrow she was dreaming about yesterday! She verbalized her dream and drowned her fears. She talked herself out of the cycle of defeat and talked herself through into her miracle!

The word of God must come to us in the power of the Holy Spirit. It must impact the person in this manner so that drastic changes can come deep within that life.

> John 1:1-4
> *"In the beginning was the Word, and the Word was with God, and the Word was God. He was in the beginning with God. All*

things came into being through Him, and apart from Him nothing came into being that has come into being. In Him was life, and the life was the Light of men."

In the word is life and the life of the word is the light of men. We will not know where to go or which direction to take if the life of the word does not hit us deeply. Many people hear a sermon, but they don't hear and touch the life of the word. That is why nothing has come into their being and into their life. Apart from the word, nothing divine or invisible will come into the physical realm. The word is the medium through which the invisible spiritual realm can be made manifest into the physical realm. When the word comes to us, it will set us free. When the word becomes flesh, we will behold God's glory and every darkness and satanic force will not have power to shut it down from coming into fulfilment.

There are three major results that happen to every believer because of the word.

Mark 4:24a
"Take care 'what you listen to' ..."

Luke 8:18
"Take care 'how you listen' ..."

Genesis 3:11
"Take care 'who tells you' ..."

Take Care What We Listen To As It Will Change Our Nature

What we listen to will shape and fashion our nature. Those who hear or heed the word of God will partake divine nature *(2 Pet 1:4)*. Those who partake words of lies and deception will develop a lying and deceptive nature.

Take Care How We Listen As It Will Determine The Depth The Word Abides In Us

How we listen will determine how deep the words will go in order to bring change within us. If we are casual with the word and let it fall by the wayside the devil will come to steal the word. If we sow it into good ground it will yield a harvest!

Romans 10:17
"Keep hearing and hearing until faith arises in your heart."

Take Care Who Instructs And Leads Us As They Will Determine Our Direction And Destiny

Whoever instructs us in life as our primary source will determine our course and destiny in life. Whoever instructs us with truth, will lead the course concerning our journey in life. Those who have been given that place of bieing our instructor, teacher and leader; will guide us into where they are going. Thus our destiny and course of action in the future will be determined by our present leaders.

Matthew 24:4
And Jesus answered and said to them, "See to it that no one misleads you.

Those who have been given authority to lead us will determine our future direction and destiny. Be determined to choose and follow accurate leaders, as our lives are too precious to be wasted by destructive leadership styles.

God has to raise strong leaders who can minister the word accurately to us and who will set the word into the pathway of fulfilment. The proceeding word must not only leave the mouth of God but must bring the reality of its fulfilment here before our eyes!

What will happen when the word is accurately ministered to someone? What divine process does the word take in the lives of its hearers? What is the pathway of the spirit connecting us to the word, its content, its dynamics and its ultimate fulfilment? There are twelve simple stages in which the word is outworked in our lives. Understanding this divine process of the spoken word will give us better clarity on how to benefit from every word that proceeded from His mouth. This divine process will change the nature of the person, renew his thinking patterns, de-program him to break every limitation and re-program him to enjoy the fullness of its reality.

When we understand the way of the Spirit, we will see the fulfilment of every word spoken to us by God. This process to outwork the proceeding word will accelerate the fulfilment of the prophecies and promises we have received from God.

> Isaiah 55:11
> *"So will My word be which goes forth from My mouth; It will not return to Me empty, Without accomplishing what I desire, And without succeeding in the matter for which I sent it."*

The Process Of Establishing Truth In The Inward Parts (12 Steps)

> 1 Corinthians 2:1
> *"And when I came to you, brethren, I did not come with superiority of speech or of wisdom, proclaiming to you the testimony of God."*

When the Apostle Paul came into Corinth he came proclaiming the testimony of what God was saying in the heavens about that Church. He carried the prophetic word of God proceeding from the mouth of God. He did not water it down with verbosity and superiority of speech. He did not contaminate God's proceeding word of life with human philosophy or with the wisdom of man. He was determined to know nothing else among them except that which can be made available to them through all who Jesus is and everything He has done for them through the Cross. It did not matter what had happened in their past and where their lineage and ancestors came from. It did not matter if their ancestors flew around on the broom or were mere cannibals. As they decided to yield to the power that was available through Paul today, it will make all the difference in their lives from that day on.

The Apostle Paul knew that his message and preaching must bring about the demonstration of the Holy Spirit and power so that their faith can rest on the power of God and not on the wisdom or wickedness of men!

When the words come in apostolic grace and in the demonstration of the Holy Spirit it will build them up and give them an inheritance among those who are sanctified.

> Acts 20:32
> *"'And now I commend you to God and to the word of grace, which is able to build you up and to give you the inheritance among all those who are sanctified.'"*

When we speak on earth what God is saying in the heavens to those who are hearing attentively and in faith, the processes of truth invasion and transformation take place. Let us study the process of the transformation of character through the power of the truth that is delivered.

A. The Reception Of Truth

1. Truth delivered is now received through our five senses as we hear what God is speaking through His Spirit.

2. However, we must be spiritually inclined and tuned to receive this frequency of truth into our hearts.

3. We must realize that we cannot receive all that we are hearing but only a part and in parts. Get the rest of the message and listen to it attentively again and again through the CDs or books available!

4. We are receiving through imperfect and incomplete sources therefore we need to properly process the message we are hearing in the power of the Spirit of truth.

These four aspects will position us to receive the best of God's word into the best of the soil in our hearts. There will be no hindrance to the reception as we have put ourselves in the pathway of the Spirit of truth flowing through these vessel of honour.

B. The Perception Of Truth

1. We must receive the truth ministered into our spirit and not lock it out into our mind. The mind can reject or choke the truth from its expression.

2. We must receive the spiritual ability to discern the contents of what we are hearing and only receive what is of the Holy Spirit.

3. We must receive understanding in our minds as to what the Holy Spirit is saying, and interpret truth with the light we are receiving from the Holy Spirit's inspiration.

4. We must keep our minds continually opened to receive insights and clarity of understanding. Any fresh new thoughts that can enlighten what we are hearing must be welcomed.

At the Perception of Truth stage, our minds will piece together what the Holy Spirit is saying. It will cause our minds to be enlightened with truth

and light. The mind must not reject the light, but yield to the light of God that is coming into it.

Psalms 119:130
"The unfolding of Your words gives light; It gives understanding to the simple."

C. The Revelation Of Truth

1. At this stage the Holy Spirit will throw light on what we are receiving and will inspire our spirit with fresh life.

2. Our spirit will be energized with God life and will come into a place of wellbeing. Our spirit will know a surge of freshness and strength.

3. When truth comes into our spirit, there is spiritual conception of the invisible and the supernatural material of creative life is within us. The word received into our spirit becomes cemented together to become the material for fulfilment of God's word.

4. The spirit and the mind are beginning to coordinate with the explosion of God-life in the spirit and spontaneous thought in the mind.

At the Revelation of Truth stage, the Holy Spirit is inspiring our spirit and refreshing it with divine light. This enlightens the thoughts of the mind. The two faculties are now being aligned as they carry the same word and are experiencing the same work of the Holy Spirit.

Hosea 9:11
"As for Ephraim, their glory will fly away like a bird-- No birth, no pregnancy and no conception!"

D. The Resolution Of Truth

1. At this stage the inspired spirit is laying hold of our minds gaining its full attention. The truth is being accepted as a resolution! The mind is yielding to the presence of fresh truth inside it.

2. The convictions of the Holy Spirit are being received and strongly felt within our spirit.

3. These spirit convictions will bring greater clarity in the mind and will redesign the thinking patterns, broadening its horizon and perspectives.

4. The unrenewed mind often struggles with conflicting thoughts from within itself. These seeds from the past experiences will try to cloud out what God is beginning to show us but the Holy Spirit's conviction will override these confusing thoughts within the mind.

At the Resolution of Truth stage, it is necessary for stronger convictions of the Spirit to become established. The Apostle must minister powerfully in the preaching anointing and inject God-life into the hearers' spirits without compromise. The minds of the hearers are now opening up other areas of their mind to reason with what is being sent into this faculty.

> Proverbs 15:2
> *"The tongue of the wise makes knowledge acceptable, But the mouth of fools spouts folly."*

These inner struggles within the mind can be silenced when wisdom to articulate and power to reason becomes the apostle's persuasive tools of ministry. Paul was reasoning and persuading them continually for three months in Ephesus *(Acts 19:8)*. The minister must keep this measure of the Spirit's grace upon the hearers as all men go through these stages of truth.

E. The Conclusion Of Truth

1. At this stage certain areas of our thoughts are being challenged and resistance is rising from unexpected areas we never thought existed in our minds.

2. The objects and areas of resistance are being revealed and are duly challenged.

3. The deception in those areas with its prejudice and inaccurate thinking pattern is arrested. We are coming out of our lies and our grey areas of compromise.

4. There is a renewing of thought pattern in those areas that have been challenged. Limited boundaries in these thinking paradigms are being replaced with new thoughts from the Holy Spirit.

At the Conclusion of Truth stage, a new possibility thinking is emerging in our minds. Those strongholds, speculations and lofty things that exalt itself within our minds, are now brought down into obedience.

These areas which have been founded in compromise and inaccuracy are now free from oppression. There is a greater freedom to think thoughts that are God-ward and liberating. There is a freshness in these areas of the mind which were formerly set in cycles of defeat. Now we agree to what is being said; we know it is from God and is true.

F. The Confirmation Of Truth

1. At this stage a choice is now made willingly because truth has become a strong conviction within our hearts.

2. We see a clearer future breakthrough because faith actions can now be implemented without restrictions and resistances from our mind and soul.

3. A new courage to move forward grips our heart and we realize that we are being activated with a new energy and inspiration for advancement.

4. We are now positioned to carry out and implement what we believe. We know a new sense of authority and positioning to execute orders.

> Ecclesiastes 8:5
> *"He who keeps a royal command experiences no trouble, for a wise heart knows the proper time and procedure."*

At the Confirmation of Truth stage, we are being positioned to act and a willingness to obey has been achieved within our faculties. We are receiving grace to carry out what we have received from above. There is a new courage because of the possibility thinking that we have become empowered to move forward and must implement what, "we have been instructed." This inspiration drives our obedience. The vision of a better future motivates us to act in faith.

> Mark 5:27-28
> *"after hearing about Jesus, she came up in the crowd behind Him and touched His cloak. For she thought, "If I just touch His garments, I will get well.""*

G. The Affirmation Of Truth

1. At this stage, the discipline and devotion of the will to act out and obey the truth received into the heart are applied diligently.

2. We are staying on the decisions we have made, without compromise as we want to see through our obedience to the Lord.

3. During this transition time of testing, our hearts are purified and our motives are purged. Here we choose to put to death the power of the flesh and the deeds of the body so that we can live by doing what God has commanded us.

4. We have chosen what is profitable not just what is lawful. We do not just obey for blessings and benefits, but rather for a higher cause of honouring Him and our convictions.

At the Affirmation of Truth, we are committed to the course of continued obedience.

> John 8:31-32
> *"So Jesus was saying to those Jews who had believed Him, "If you continue in My word, then you are truly disciples of Mine; and you will know the truth, and the truth will make you free.""*

These times of testing proves our commitment to carry out His word in our lives. Our initial motives and desires for personal benefits and blessings are replaced by a higher attitude to honour Him. God releases greater wisdom in our hearts as we realize a new dimension of life that is now available to us. We can live in a place of freedom to choose a higher order of life. Even though we could choose a lower standard, we are now more determined to do our best for His glory!

H. The Application Of Truth

1. At this stage we are seen persistently practicing the human will in applying the truth. We resist the temptation to slow down our pace of obedience.

2. We meditate on the word to find deeper clarity to what God is saying. We find more meaningful ways to carry out these truths.

3. We discover to our amazement that others before us have already succeeded in applying the same truth in their own lives. This will inspire us to obey and live it out in our generation.

4. This will allow fresh wisdom to come upon our hearts to build accurately into our lives the truths we have received.

At the Application of Truth, the key of meditation quickens God's wisdom to give us plans and strategies to carry out this word accurately. In meditation we not only know that "God has spoken," but also that, "the One who has spoken is God!"

Biologically speaking, food is not in our body until it has been absorbed into our bloodstream. There is a lot of truth that we believe that never becomes part of our lives because we do not meditate on the process of how to take them into our hearts and minds. Through this process these words can become written in our minds and our hearts.

> Hebrews 10:16
> *""THIS IS THE COVENANT THAT I WILL MAKE WITH THEM AFTER THOSE DAYS, SAYS THE LORD: I WILL PUT MY LAWS UPON THEIR HEART, AND ON THEIR MIND I WILL WRITE THEM," He then says,"*

The more we meditate, the more our minds are set upon the things of the Holy Spirit. Our minds will discover ways of application that we never saw was possible. Our minds will understand the depth of truth that we never thought we would know. We will sense that outworking these truths will bring about a new lifestyle of meaningful intimacy with God.

I. The Assimilation Of Truth

1. At this stage we are choosing to form consistent habits and patterns around the truth we have received and have now come to believe.

2. We are consistently seeking opportunities to practice these dimensions of truth.

3. We will begin to see a change in our nature and character that reflects the influence of the truths we are receiving from God, on our lives.

4. When the truth has become a consistent habit, a whole new world opens up before us. God is now getting us ready to move into a new sphere of life.

At the Assimilation of Truth stage, habits are being formed because of the truth and around the truth we have received. God equips us with the necessary tools and dimensions in the spirit to activate these truths and bless others with our lives. This area of truth will spearhead other areas of our spirit growth.

J. The Transformation Of Truth

1. At this stage we are manifesting a new nature that reflects the life and spirit of these truths.

2. We are manifesting obedience and trust in God's word in accordance to this truth that has been revealed to us.

3. We have now gained divine knowledge and our confidence in this area of truth is exemplary.

4. This subject of truth has become clearer to us and other passages of Scripture relating to this truth begins to unfold itself with ease. Other scriptures are unlocking each other on the basis of the revealed truth which we have already received.

At this Transformation of Truth stage, we receive a new identity even with those who see us daily, because the truth that is affecting us, is revealing its nature and character through us. It's becoming evident that we have not only received and believed this truth, but that it is becoming our life and core value.

We are becoming transformed from one level of glory to another level and it is now becoming a nature within us. We have not learnt this truth from men, but through God who is now exploding through us in the nature of what has been sown into our hearts. The evidence that the word is now living in us is undeniable.

K. The Revolution Of Truth

1. At this stage we are now living the kingdom core values and living this truth centred life providing an alternative lifestyle for others to follow after.

2. We are revealing God's way and pattern through our lives. People can read in and through our lives, how God is outworking a pattern and a process by these truths.

3. We are now modelling the message and have become the living epistles for all men to read and know.

4. We are God's light and truth, revealing His ways and His righteousness. God can reach men around us faster as He is visibly manifesting through our lives before their eyes. People do not always read the Bible but they do read the lives of those who do!

At the Revolution of Truth stage, the message received is now becoming loud and clear in the expression of a human life. People do not always change because they read the Bible; people change because change is all around them. The most powerful message is not hidden in a book, it is spoken through a life. We need to see the relevance of the Bible in the human lives that believe it.

Thousands are waiting in line for this revolution of truth and the revolution of values to begin through our lives. They must testify how truth has set us free. They need to know that it has power to bring change and abundance of life. They need to see us if they would truly believe!

L. The Impartation Of Truth

1. At this final stage we multiply our lives into the lives of others because the life of the truth is living in us. We reproduce ourselves into the lives of others.

Acts 6:7

"The word of God kept on spreading; and the number of the disciples continued to increase greatly in Jerusalem, and a great many of the priests were becoming obedient to the faith."

Acts 12:24

"But the word of the Lord continued to grow and to be multiplied."

Acts 19:20

"So the word of the Lord was growing mightily and prevailing."

2. God is now giving us a stature to impart this life of truth we are modeling, into the lives of others.

3. God is multiplying the word and it is continuing to increase and prevail among the people.

4. The word has become flesh and is dwelling among us. People will receive grace and truth from what we are continually modelling in our life.

At the final stage of the Impartation of Truth, we are bringing to completion the full cycle of where the word needs to operate in. It must be modeled in flesh and blood. All the confusion and inaccurate understandings will be removed when it is accurately being modelled in a human life.

John 1:14

"And the Word became flesh, and dwelt among us, and we saw His glory, glory as of the only begotten from the Father, full of grace and truth."

John 1:16-17

"For of His fullness we have all received, and grace upon grace. For the Law was given through Moses; grace and truth were realized through Jesus Christ."

When the Word becomes flesh and blood, we are bringing the word from the invisible realm into the material realm. This word will become the life and light of men and darkness will not have power to shut its operation out. When the word of God is modeled in human lives, these lives become the living epistles.

When we continue to move deeper into living these truths, we carry grace and truth for those around us. Those who hear our lives and not just our messages will receive the truth we have modeled in our lives. Since these truths have been lived through human lives, the essence and spirit of truth flowing through us will set them free. They are both set free from what is holding them and empowered by grace to do what is needed for them to move forward into total victory.

God has intended for us to not just be hearers of the word but also to become doers of the word *(James 1:22)*.

Those who are doers of the word, are instructed to teach *(Acts 1:1)* and instruct others. We can teach on any subject, but we can only impart that which we are. Thus, the impartation of truth is the only way whereby lives will be fully transformed and changed. The pattern Son, Jesus, has shown us how to model truth and life for all men to know the way!

Summary:

A. Reception of Truth: I am hearing what is being said.

B. Perception of Truth: I am receiving the things said.

C. Revelation of Truth: I understand what I am receiving.

D. Resolution of Truth: I am processing what I am agreeing.

E. Conclusion of Truth: I agree with God, His Word is true.

F. Confirmation of Truth: I believe now so I will speak.

G. Affirmation of Truth: I will do it as I believe it.

H. Application of Truth: I am implementing the process.

I. Assimilation of Truth: I am practicing a habit.

J. Transformation of Truth: I am modelling a lifestyle.

K. Revolution of Truth: I am influencing lives.

L. Impartation of Truth: I am reproducing myself into other lives.

Truth modelled by a life is truth lived to its fullest!

Chapter Ten

Moving Believers To The Next Level Of Maturity

When the Apostle Paul arrived in Ephesus he found some disciples of Apollos. He evaluated their spiritual foundations as a wise master builder and found that they were lacking. In today's evaluation they would not even have met the standards of being an Evangelical believer.

Like their leader, Apollos, they were only acquainted with the baptism of John *(Acts 18:24-26)*. The Lord Jesus had come, had died, had risen and ascended to the Father. The church had come forth in the power of the Holy Spirit and ministry gifts had been released upon the scene. Yet, this fervent and eloquent preacher was still speaking and teaching the past revelations, totally ignorant of the progressive revelation of what God is saying and doing in his days.

The scenario is not different today as there are huge numbers of ministers and ministries who are still peddling in the past outdated irrelevant teachings. Unfortunately, they seem to have large followings too. Their disciples are at the same spiritual level as their leaders. The current apostolic move is to bring everyone into the present day progressive truth which God is revealing. Those who received the word can be brought into the apostolic community and become devoted to the apostle doctrine *(Acts 2:41-42)*.

When the Apostle Paul found these "left behind" disciples, he started to work with them. Priscilla and Aquila took Apollos aside and explained to him the way of God more accurately *(Acts 18:26).* The apostolic is about the more excellent way *(1 Cor 12:31b).*

This chapter will cover the essence of this concept of moving believers to the next level of maturity so that they are not left behind in knowledge, experience or relevance in society.

There are five levels of spiritual maturity within the church today. Understanding these levels will allow Pastors to grow the believers to the next level. We must move them through the spiritual processes and help them transit into the next level. We must not allow them to settle at the lowest levels, but wean them out of it into pursuing maturity.

> Hebrews 6:1-3
> *"Therefore leaving the elementary teaching about the Christ, let us press on to maturity, not laying again a foundation of repentance from dead works and of faith toward God, of instruction about washings and laying on of hands, and the resurrection of the dead and eternal judgment. And this we will do, if God permits."*

The elementary teachings are basic essential core values that establish our foundation in Christ. Without being established on the foundation of Christ we will not be allowed or permitted to go forward.

Walking in the foundation of Christ allows us to have access into:

- The dimensions of life and gifts of the Holy Spirit *(Heb 6:4-5).*
- The pure word of truth from the throne *(Heb 12:25).*
- The victory over sin in our lives. God will give us the victory and bring the sin age to an end in our own lives. The days of struggle over sin, sickness and satan will be brought to an end.

- We receive a kingdom that cannot be shaken or taken *(Heb 12:28)*. God will establish His Kingdom rule over the nations through the church *(Acts 2:34, 35, Heb 10:12-13)*.

- God will bring us into maturity of stature and to a perfected state of the church. Zion will become a reality on earth where God will dwell amongst His holy people. This is the city God promised the Old Testament patriarchs and saints *(Heb 11:16)*.

We must lead every believer to membership functions and then move them forward to true discipleship functions. We then take them to another level of leadership functions as ministers of the House of God. We must lead the ministers in the House from ministry functions into a greater level of stature and maturity as sons and teach them to acquire the ownership and inheritance of the House. This ownership function and mentality will allow them to function effectively until they possess their inheritance in the House. Let us deal in detail with the five levels of maturity in the House.

Level One – The Believers

The believer is one who is truly born again by the word of the Kingdom *(Matt 13:19)* and his eyes can see the Kingdom *(Jn 3:3)*.

He has received the word of the Kingdom and not just the goodness or gospel of the benefits of salvation. (Come to Jesus and be saved. Come to Him and He will give you peace. Receive your healing and forgiveness. You are now saved from hell etc.) All these are statements concerning the benefits of the Kingdom which God graciously and abundantly gives to those who choose the Kingdom of God. The believer must know that he has now become the subject of the Kingdom and must choose to live under the domain of the King. He must choose to pursue God until he is in the Kingdom, and lives under the domain and covering of the King.

Distinctive Features Of A Believer

A believer in the church can be identified by these five features below:

- Often, he is only interested in his personal relationship with God. He is born again and he desires to know his God and spends time pursuing Him.

- He enjoys the benefits of salvation and finds every way to receive as much of these benefits as possible. He desires to find access into all that is his. He also longs to improve his personal happiness in this life.

- His perspectives in the word are often personalized. Everything is read from his viewpoint of personal perspectives. "What is in there for me and how can it help me further my cause in this life?" becomes a compelling force.

- His prayer life is also centred around himself and his needs as he is pushing his faith to see God come through for him. This is the testimony he is building for himself as the quality of faith of the believer is often decided by how fast he can get God to respond by meeting his personal needs and desires.

- His mentality is established on receiving personal edification for personal achievement. Believers enter into any service wanting to be blessed and receive their own edification. It does not occur in their minds that they should be a blessing in the service to touch lives of others.

This framework of thought and paradigm prevents the believer from walking into maturity. The self-centredness and pursuit of personal blessings prevent many from entering a corporate lifestyle. Their narrow view that "all things must benefit me," prevents them from considering other people's needs. This makes it impossible for them to consider helping, or getting involved in the church unless they see any clear benefit or profit for themselves. This selfish perspective is not only seen in those who have just come into new birth, but also even in others who have been in church for a long time. It is embarrassing to note that this is also the case in much of the church leadership today. A person who is at this level of maturity as a believer can be found in different positions of the church hierarchy today. This is because we allowed the people to climb up towards the pinnacle of success and spiritual responsibility too quickly without first proving them before promoting them.

There are so many in the ranks and files of the church with a strong believers mentality saturated in self-centredness and who are extremely personal in their perspectives.

Level Two – The Members

The member is one who has come to his senses and remembers his father's house *(Luke 15:17)*. The son has come to his senses and he is now desirous to come home into the father's house and family. Those who are believers must be brought into the true process of repentance so that they can become integrated for interaction within the family.

The prodigal son in *Luke 15:*

- Came to the end of his ways *(v. 14)*.
- Came to his senses *(v. 17)*.
- Came to the father *(v. 18)*.
- Came to the father's house *(v.20)*.
- Came to the father's family *(v. 21-24)*.
- Came to the father's other son *(v. 25)*.
- Came to his true inheritance *(v. 22)*.

Distinctive Features Of A Member

A member can be identified by the following five features:

- He has discovered the church is his home not just God's house. The church has become his reference point and has become his meeting point. He now has an address in his Christian walk as a believer.

- He is beginning to understand that he must embrace a corporate lifestyle not just a personal devotion to Christ. He realizes that he is born again into a family and now sees the need to belong to a larger identity in the community of believers. He must loose the selfish personal expressions that can frustrate the corporate lifestyle.

- He is now willing to pay the price to adjust his personal lifestyle and becomes ready to make sacrifices for a common destiny with the people he now feels a sense of belonging to. He is now prepared to rush home from work to attend the church meeting or travel out to a home group outside his neighbourhood. He is prepared to make adjustments to his time and his lifestyle including his spending habits so that he can fulfill his responsibility in the corporate lifestyle he has now chosen.

- He respects the authority chain God has put over the House of God and he is prepared to willingly submit his life under this oversight. He is now seeing the need to be under the covering of God's authority which is now distributed to those whom God has chosen and appointed on his behalf. The member is willing to allow the Set Man in the House to speak into his life, to counsel and coach him to maturity.

- He has identified himself with this kingdom community which he has now also chosen to be identified with. He has chosen them as his family and desire to know and relate meaningfully with them. He desires to stand together with them and represent them honourably. He has chosen to live out the family distinctives and express the family culture and core values in his lifestyle and speech. This expression of the similarities of the group makes him an unashamed part of this family.

Many leaders and pastors do not even walk in this level of maturity as they constantly collide with the appointed Set Man in the house. Many refuse to submit their lives, their decisions and their core values to the delegated authority of those whom God has appointed to watch over their souls. How many there are, being in this stage or state of maturity who have crossed over into leadership roles and functions, is anybody's guess. Many of the pioneer leaders of our churches have allowed the "Hagar type" of leadership into our midst. Anyone who can promise to deliver, and anyone who has personality and charisma to hold a position of authority became our immediate choice for leadership. When the church starts to grow, we realize that we are trying to bring God's word into fulfilment through these alternative vessels we have chosen, but who are not chosen by the Lord. The curse of the wrong choices of the Hagar type leadership is wrecking churches today and it will continue to destroy churches in the future. Man, in his desperateness, is choosing anything and everyone whom the Lord has not chosen to become leaders. They are now spearheading what the Lord has commissioned us to do.

Level Three – The Disciples

The basic raw material for apostolic ministry is a disciple. We need more disciples than devotees or converts if the church is to fulfil Kingdom purposes.

> Matthew 28:19
> *""Go therefore and make disciples of all the nations, baptizing them in the name of the Father and the Son and the Holy Spirit,"*

The apostolic commission was not a mandate for every believer or every church member. It was an assignment for disciples who have walked with the Master for three and a half years!

We cannot disciple anyone if we have not been discipled ourselves. If God has not raised anyone to form the pattern into us, how then do we have the right to form the lives of others? If we do not know the pattern, how then do we build and form lives in the nations?

Many preachers are running to and fro across the earth with a message they have not model in their own lives. The message and the messenger must become one in order for the Holy Spirit to bring impact upon the hearers.

> 2 Corinthians 4:2b
> *""but by the manifestation of truth commending ourselves to every man's conscience in the sight of God.""*

It means that when we speak the message the Holy Spirit will speak into their spirit and vouch for us as being true. God will attest to them with many convincing proofs that we are sent of the Lord to them. God will bear witness in their conscience that we are of the truth.

A disciple is one who models his belief and behaviour systems after the life of his master in order to become like him and represent him fully.

A disciple is not above his teacher in authority or in stature, but a disciple must become like his teacher for he has the potential to be like the one he is following. The highest level of discipleship is seen when he becomes the head of the house and raises a whole new generation of disciples to imitate him as he imitates his teacher.

> Matthew 10:24-25
> *""A disciple is not above his teacher, nor a slave above his master. "It is enough for the disciple that he become like his teacher, and the slave like his master. If they have called the head of the house Beelzebul, how much more will they malign the members of his household!"*

There are very few models of discipleship in society today because of individualistic philosophies centred on selfishness. The closest example illustrating discipleship I can relate to is found in the ancient times among those who were pioneers in the martial arts of self-defense. This is the nearest example to true discipleship of biblical value for us today.

Distinctive Features Of A Disciple

The following are five important and distinctive features in a true disciple:

- A disciple is willing to embrace the truth he is taught and live it out as his lifestyle. He is not a hearer of the word deceiving himself, but rather a doer of the word. He is prepared for, and live to exemplify what his teacher teaches. He wants to become the living epistles of his teacher *(2 Cor 3:2-3)*. He models the core values of the one whom he follows.

  Many in our churches do not live for the purpose of modelling our message and living it out as a letter of recommendation for the pastor's ministry. We need to model the message packaged in the human lives who have chosen to represent us fully.

- He is willing to change his current thinking pattern to follow the fresh truth that is presented to him. A devotee is set on the old that he has learned and he will be faithful to it till the end. Like the Apostle Peter, he will have misgivings when a new revelation and present truth is revealed to him. He will polarize to the past point of reference (in this case Moses and the commandments) and fight the new revelation and the Revealer *(Acts 10:10-20)*. Sometimes Peter's personal preferences became the deciding factor in his obedience (or lack of it) to God.

  A devotee specializes in reproducing the past rituals and procedures of the human traditions whereas a disciple is prepared to stay abreast with the knowledge of his teacher.

- A disciple has a leader from whom he is drawing his source of truth. A disciple does not draw from everywhere and from everyone. He is clear who his leader is and draws from that primary source. With this criteria we can now determine how many disciples we have in our churches. Church folks are into every seminar and conference. Some of them are so gullible and undiscerning that they eat everything that is served without any ability to filter out the deception and inaccurate doctrines.

A pastor is blessed when he has disciples in his church who follow what he is teaching and who become connected to the same source as their teacher. Then their frequencies will become tuned to receive from the same broadcasting station as he is receiving. His investment into these lives will pay off as they will not be wavering in what they believe, but implement what they have been instructed to do.

- A disciple observes and duplicates the way of his leader even though he is still a disciple. The disciple starts to follow the pace and passion of his leader at an early age and accelerates in his growth. He trains to become like his master and works at being at his best in the footsteps of the master. He is passionate about reproducing the way and works of his master even at his early years so that he can represent him well and bring praise to the master. This attitude and spirit of excellence in the disciple will cause the master to be honoured by his achievement at his young age. It is because of the disciples like the above that masters are honoured by others.

We have yet to see this calibre of the disciples who will so impress the society that they will bring honour to the Pastors who have raised them in the house. The days of the new generation are here and this honour is for the Set Man of the house who raises his sons and daughters accurately for the Kingdom.

- A disciple enters into the same ministry and primary assignment as that which God has assigned to the Set Man of the house. For a true disciple there is only one life to follow and one ministry to reproduce and that is the one of the supreme leader! Unlike the Charismatic understanding of, "serving until we are ready to make it on our own," philosophy!

Luke 16:12
""And if you have not been faithful in the use of that which is another's, who will give you that which is your own?"

If we have not been faithfully and honourably serving the ministry of the Set Man whom God has appointed over us how will God give us ownership and possession of what we are serving under. This thought is consistent with the lives of Moses and Joshua, Samuel and David, Elijah and Elisha, Jesus and the apostles and also Paul and Timothy. God will not allow us to inherit that which God has given to those above us if that is what we personally despise.

The disciple does not want to be anybody else, but to be like his teacher. He will desire to continue what his master began in his life and generation. The disciple will desire to bring the memory of his master into his generation by living out the master's life, his works and his core values. The master will then be remembered through the lives of his disciples.

The church is often is lacking when it comes to true discipleship and the ability to reproduce men and women in succession.

> Ecclesiastes 2:16
> *"For there is no lasting remembrance of the wise man as with the fool, inasmuch as in the coming days all will be forgotten. And how the wise man and the fool alike die!"*

There will be no lasting remembrance of the wise man due to the lack of accurate succession. We expect the people who come after us to continue the legacy of all that we have established for them. We desire the good work we have started to be carried on to greater heights.

We can see that the king had done a good work in his lifetime *(Ecc 2:4-10)* and did more than anyone else that preceded him in Jerusalem. His expectation was for someone to continue to carry on his legacy to become an enduring work in the future.

> Ecclesiastes 2:18-21
> *"Thus I hated all the fruit of my labor for which I had labored under the sun, for I must leave it to the man who will come after me. And who knows whether he will be a wise man or a fool? Yet he will have control over all the fruit of my labor for which I have labored by acting wisely under the sun. This too is vanity.*

Therefore I completely despaired of all the fruit of my labor for which I had labored under the sun. When there is a man who has labored with wisdom, knowledge and skill, then he gives his legacy to one who has not labored with them. This too is vanity and a great evil."

The great evil and vanity he saw in his day is the same as what we are seeing today. The legacy must be left behind to the man who will come after us. If he is wise and has laboured with wisdom, knowledge and skill as we have in our life then the legacy continues with this man. But if he is a fool, then he will squander all that we have laboured for and built at the expense of our lives.

The major reason for this chapter is to be able to identify the spiritual maturity of our people so that we will be able to use them appropriately in the building of the house of God. Often what we built becomes destroyed by the ensuing generations. Let wisdom prevail among the builders of His House. We need to see the basic requirements of discipleship in the church so that we can be sure we have the raw materials to transfer legacy. Most pastors have not come up to address this concern as many are not building a legacy to be transferred in succession. They are quite happy to have believers and members since that will be sufficient to pay the bills and continue the routine running of the programs and activities of the church.

The maturity level of the church must be at the discipleship level so that we can start the apostolic process of city taking and national transformation.

Acts 19:1
"It happened that while Apollos was at Corinth, Paul passed through the upper country and came to Ephesus, and found some disciples."

These disciples of Apollos were upgraded and updated. They were filled with the Holy Spirit and were entrusted with the gifts of the Spirit. These disciples were receiving apostolic input that transformed their nature and made them become vessels Paul could use to take the city.

Acts 19:7
"There were in all about twelve men."

The disciples were being changed and they became vessels Paul could use. They could be counted on. The true apostolic church was now beginning to arise in Ephesus. Do not leave the church on the first two levels of maturity as they are insufficient levels for the church to take on an apostolic position in the city. Most mega churches today do not have true disciples who can reproduce what they hear and see in their leaders.

Level Four – The Ministers

It is only at this level of maturity that spiritual responsibility can be given to those within the house. We are not talking about "one another" responsibilities but responsibilities that carry authority and government in the house. One another responsibilities are like encouraging one another, submitting to one another, taking meals together, sharing with one another, etc. These are done to fulfil our commitment to the covenant community. They are responsibilities that are carried out as a faithful member of the body. We fulfil our functions by supplying "according to the proper working of each individual part, causing growth of the whole body ..." *(Eph. 4:16)*.

A minister is one who is responsible for accurate implementation of the decrees that have been decided on by the king who is exercising accurate government through the minister's rulership. In essence, a minister is one who helps implement accurate government within the church by his role function as an appointed representative of the Set Man. He contributes his skills, talents, graces, gifts and anointings to help accelerate the implementation of all that is needed to bring the desires of the Set Man into fulfilment.

The ministers in the house are not just people who are ministering what they want and what they are gifted in. They have to accurately use what they have with the purpose of fulfilling the mandate God has given to the Set Man of the house. This differs from the concept of just doing what we can. It involves

honing our skills, talents and graces so that we can help bring the corporate community into their prophetic destiny.

For Joshua to fulfil his mandate to bring the people of God into possession of the land, he needed to have men he could command to carry out his instructions which are part of his strategy in leadership.

> Joshua 1:6
> *""Be strong and courageous, for you shall give this people possession of the land which I swore to their fathers to give them."*
>
> Joshua 1:10
> *"Then Joshua commanded the officers of the people, saying,"*
>
> Joshua 1:16-18
> *"They answered Joshua, saying, "All that you have commanded us we will do, and wherever you send us we will go. "Just as we obeyed Moses in all things, so we will obey you; only may the LORD your God be with you as He was with Moses. "Anyone who rebels against your command and does not obey your words in all that you command him, shall be put to death; only be strong and courageous.""*

Distinctive Features Of A Minister

There are five features that highlight the role functions of ministers in the house.

- A minister is one who functions and contributes his grace to the overall edification of the church. He tailors what he has to be in maximum capacity so that he can perform well to move the people forward in their pursuit of destiny. He uses all that he has and turbo charges the church to leap forward into what God has desired for them. The minister contributes in such a way to accelerate growth of the whole body.

Ephesians 4:16

"from whom the whole body, being fitted and held together by what every joint supplies, according to the proper working of each individual part, causes the growth of the body for the building up of itself in love."

In short, his involvement accelerates the people to move forward by creating a synergy in the spirit among them. The ministry of the word, the operation of the gifts, the ministry of a psalmist etc. can all inspire the church into a new level towards what God desires the church to move into.

- A minister is one defined by his function and not necessarily by his position. The current church is not only heavy into titles, but also into non-functioning hierarchical positions. These men carry a title or position without providing it justice by accurately functioning in its role. If by calling an apostle by his title will release him to function accurately, let's call them as such. But we know, calling someone according to his ministry grace is not the key to moving the man into the operation of it. We, nevertheless, function in the grace whether someone calls us as such or not. We need to know that what we carry, and function accurately in it because of His grace. The people will know when they see a genuine ministry in operation in the Spirit. They will recognize that the Lord is with us and this would be a better testimony bringing glory to Him, rather than one that draws all the attention to our persona!

- A minister is one who operates in the spirit of excellence to provide peak performance because he realizes he is but a steward of God's grace and gifting. A minister understands he is called to faithfulness and that he must employ every faculty of his life to bring the best for the people to whom he is assigned as minister. The minister of the government, who is a member of a parliament, knows that he must serve the people of his constituency well as he represents the government to them. Any shortcomings on his side will reflect on the wisdom of the government for choosing one who is not well able to represent them accurately and one who does not have what it takes to bring good governance into implementation over their lives. In short, he has no power to deliver the promise of the implementation of the policies.

The minister in the church represents the Set Man as a member of the Set Man's governance. By using what he has and performing well, he brings true appreciation for the Set Man's life and ministry into the congregation.

- A minister functions under the authority of the Set Man and learns to live in total accountability for what he has been entrusted with. A minister knows his boundary and will operate honourably in what has been given to him. He knows that what he has, was given him by those who appointed him. He knows that the authority he has, was given to him because he has come under the authority of the Set Man. Those who are honourable understand that there must be accurate accounting of the role functions that has been given. To abuse that role and find leverage through those functions would be total lack of wisdom. Why would we need to steal what we have been freely given? Why would we need to keep some for ourselves when we have always been provided for by those above us? A minister is an honourable servant and not a thief! Remember there is no honour among thieves.

- A minister in the house captures the heart of the owner of the ministry. This ability to know the heart and mind of the Set Man of the house will allows us to have access to the grace of God in the man above us.

> 2 Kings 2:12-14
> *"Elisha saw it and cried out, "My father, my father, the chariots of Israel and its horsemen!" And he saw Elijah no more. Then he took hold of his own clothes and tore them in two pieces. He also took up the mantle of Elijah that fell from him and returned and stood by the bank of the Jordan. He took the mantle of Elijah that fell from him and struck the waters and said, "Where is the LORD, the God of Elijah?" And when he also had struck the waters, they were divided here and there; and Elisha crossed over."*

Connecting accurately to Elijah, the man of God allowed Elisha to access the God of the man. This is the secret of those who serve honourably in this generation as they are accessing the God of the man they are serving.

There is a whole new generation of ministers that will rise in the true temple and their hearts will be set apart with passion to pursue the man of God without distraction. They will follow hard after the Set Man so that they can serve the people as the man of God would want to serve them. All our ministers must press in for this level of maturity.

Often it is those who are to represent our heart and affection that sorely misrepresent us in the eyes of the people we love. This wedge is the sword of Absalom into the heart of the father and Set Man in the house. God is purging the hearts of those who are ministers in the house so that they walk circumspectly to represent the father of the house and the purpose of God through him for the city and community.

Level Five – The Sons

This is the final stage of maturity we are looking for in those who are in the House of God. The greatest asset of the church is not just its people BUT THE RIGHT PEOPLE. Churches are filled today by all kinds of people, the good, the bad, the ugly and the dirty dozen! Pastors are becoming discouraged raising a whole company of people who are totally disconnected from God and from the purposes of God in the House. Most of them are content to see that the church exists to meet them at the level of their needs and social expectations. People hold the churches at ransom by manipulating others to back their dissent and grievances over the leadership, instead of releasing and encouraging leaders to move forward into the direction God is calling the Corporate community.

At the end of the day, only sons will remain in the house to inherit what the father has laid aside as an inheritance. The prodigal son is the picture of many in current leadership today. They enjoy the benefits of the legacy and the blessings the man of God is bringing into their lives. They are glad to be in the House where all the things they desire are happening. They are blessed and are seeing their lives move into greater prosperity. Then it happens. The selfish devil rises in them. "Father, give me my share of the estate that falls to me" (and I am out of here!) *(Luke 15:12)*.

Churches throughout the nations have suffered from this plague, when those who grow in the house walk out on us taking their portion out of the house into a distant country. When this happens a spirit of discouragement and frustration hits the home base!

The brother who stayed back in the house had to pick up the pieces in all the areas the younger brother had left unattended. The worship department (Lucifer came from that department!), the cell groups, leadership functions, the administration departments or the ministry of helps are often hit by sudden disappearance of those whom we have trusted to stay. There is a huge vacuum when they leave their post on the walls of Jerusalem. The work becomes vulnerable and those who have remained faithful and have stayed are overstretched.

Interestingly, Jesus mentions that the marketplace also faces this problem of those who exploit the house in order for them to gain a share of the goods before they exit the company.

> Luke 16:1
> *"Now He was also saying to the disciples, "There was a rich man who had a manager, and this manager was reported to him as squandering his possessions."*
>
> Luke 16:4
> *"'I know what I shall do, so that when I am removed from the management people will welcome me into their homes.'"*

The unrighteous manager acted shrewdly so that he could profit in his exit out from the company when he is terminated from office. He jumped the gun on the owner of the company.

There are two practical ways to prevent this plague of Egypt from happening in our midst. The first is to raise up true sons who will stand in the line of succession like Joshua did before Moses and Elisha before Elijah. Only sons who are willing to receive their inheritance will remain loyal to the father. The "other sons of the prophets" will stand opposite them at a distance but

the true sons will crossover for succession *(2 Kings 2:7).*

The second practical way to solve this problem would be to destroy dead-end bureaucratic systems of leadership, and reproduce more labourers and leaders for every work or responsibility within the church. Reproduce two or three more for every department leader we raise. We can easily replace them if there is any departure. The apostles replaced Judas who left his office and share in the ministry with the wisdom and direction of the Holy Spirit. Amazingly, there were only two who were equally qualified to fill this gap left by Judas. We must always be ready to replace anyone who leaves the office and position given to them. Have at least two we can choose from and give it to the better of the two!

> Acts 1:17
> *""For he was counted among us and received his share in this ministry.""*
>
> Acts 1:25
> *"to occupy this ministry and apostleship from which Judas turned aside to go to his own place.""*

Dead-end bureaucratic systems of leadership allow the monopoly of leaders over entire systems in their departments. The drummer refuses to let others in, the bass guitarist stays in his role forever, the song leaders dominate the stage with their own style and it becomes their "little kingdom" into which no other aspiring person will be allowed to tread in!

Distinctive Features Of A Son

These are the seven distinctive features that are manifested in true sons in the house. Sons are what we aspire to raise and release as they will take the legacy on and bring greater achievement and advancement for the kingdom purpose in our churches. Since sonship is the ultimate goal of our instruction let us get deeper into these truths that can liberate the leaders and set them on the right cause of action for reproducing sons. God has set the pattern for

us to raise accurate sons and bring them into glory. The raising of created beings of the angelic host could not meet and fulfil the purposes of God. Thus He began to execute it through His Begotten Son the Lord Jesus Christ and then to bring it to completion through the "other sons and the church of the firstborn".

Ephesians 3:10-11
"so that the manifold wisdom of God might now be made known through the church to the rulers and the authorities in the heavenly places. This was in accordance with the eternal purpose which He carried out in Christ Jesus our Lord,"

Romans 8:29
"For those whom He foreknew, He also predestined to become conformed to the image of His Son, so that He would be the firstborn among many brethren;"

Hebrews 2:10
"For it was fitting for Him, for whom are all things, and through whom are all things, in bringing many sons to glory, to perfect the author of their salvation through sufferings."

A. Sons Are Connected To The Father Of The House In A Direct Relationship Of Covenant

Sons do not operate on a second hand relationship through a hierarchy or another chain of authority. This level of relationship of loyalty and integrity allows the sons to capture the heart and mind of the father. Fourteen years of consistently walking together, gave Elisha an insight into the heart of Elijah and what God was doing in his life. It allowed Elisha to partake the outworking of God's grace in Elijah's life. Sons are close enough to the heart and life of the Set Man to access the grace of God on his life. They are there on time and in close proximity with what God is currently doing in their father's life.

1 Chronicles 11:1-3

"Then all Israel gathered to David at Hebron and said, "Behold, we are your bone and your flesh. "In times past, even when Saul was king, you were the one who led out and brought in Israel; and the LORD your God said to you, 'You shall shepherd My people Israel, and you shall be prince over My people Israel.'" So all the elders of Israel came to the king at Hebron, and David made a covenant with them in Hebron before the LORD; and they anointed David king over Israel, according to the word of the LORD through Samuel."

David was in the fourth stage of his prophetic destiny in God. Hebron was a place of covenant making and covenant fellowship. The people came to him at that time because it was time for Israel to follow the God-appointed leader and become connected to him. God was taking him on to fulfil what He had promised him. By connecting accurately with him in covenant, they also moved on into their own destiny!

B. Sons Must Be Joined To The God Of The House

Every house and family on earth derives its name and nature from the Father in heaven. This divine nature and distinctive characteristic is released into the life of the Set Man of the house to reproduce into his tribe and family here on earth.

I.S.A.A.C. (International Strategic Alliance of Apostolic Churches) has its own distinctive feature and unique DNA because of its own Presiding Apostle and spiritual father. It is uniquely different as there is only one Jonathan David and the grace God has outworked in my life expresses differently from other apostles on the earth. We do not compare or compete, as God has graced us differently.

Galatians 2:6-9

"But from those who were of high reputation (what they were makes no difference to me; God shows no partiality)--well, those who were of reputation contributed nothing to me. But on the

contrary, seeing that I had been entrusted with the gospel to the uncircumcised, just as Peter had been to the circumcised (for He who effectually worked for Peter in his apostleship to the circumcised effectually worked for me also to the Gentiles), and recognizing the grace that had been given to me, James and Cephas and John, who were reputed to be pillars, gave to me and Barnabas the right hand of fellowship, so that we might go to the Gentiles and they to the circumcised."

To tie someone down to a certain personal opinion and expectation is due to ignorance concerning the operation of God's grace. Some men can wear a few hats in life and remain successful in all of them, while others find it difficult to operate successfully even in the one that they are wearing. Each man falls or stands before His own Maker.

Sons must connect to the grace of God and the spiritual resources in the house of their fathers. This will help them become distinctively like their father and cause them to become the begotten in the house.

Isaiah 61:9
"Then their offspring will be known among the nations, And their descendants in the midst of the peoples. All who see them will recognize them Because they are the offspring whom the LORD has blessed."

Our offsprings will be known and will become recognized among the nations because of the distinctive features. Those who see them will be able to identify them because these identifiable features of DNA, set them apart from others.

Sons in the House must tap into the spirit of what God is doing in the House. This nature of the spirit must become the nature in the lives of the son, thus they will carry the spirit of the house.

C. Sons Are Submitted To The Appointed Leaders In The House

The nature of true sons is seen as they yield to submitting to delegated authority in the house. They submit and honour the Set Man as well as those who are appointed in the leadership structure by him. They recognize these approved leaders as the extension of their father's governance and respond to them honourably. The sons in the house choose to keep unity and order for accurate government to be established in the house. They are desirous to see peace and righteousness become the foundation for the house and the lives of the people within the house.

Sons in the house are willing to be led, discipled and trained for effective roles in the house. They are prepared to be "under guardians and managers until the date set by the father" *(Gal 4:2).* Their willingness to recognize and yield to all delegated authority is because they see it as an extension of their father's authority and rulership. They yield to it because of honour for their father's rulership and stature.

Sons have a clear perception of the whole structure of the house as one living enterprise. They know that their father is connected to all the systems of operation within, and they will not resist the desires and plans of their father which are being implemented in each department. They have learned to labour alongside their father and his friends.

> Matthew 12:30
> *""He who is not with Me is against Me; and he who does not gather with Me scatters."*
>
> Mark 9:40
> *""For he who is not against us is for us."*

D. Sons Are Connected To The People Of The House

They have developed a meaningful relationship with all who are part of the house and are accurately connected to this kingdom community. They are identifying

their family and are conscious of the spiritual responsibilities towards them as they represent their father in the house. They are willing to share their life and resources because these are the people they belong to and are covenanted with. By developing this amazing wholesome relationship within the community, the body is held together and synergized for forward momentum towards destiny.

The people in the house are their companions and they draw strength from them in times of need.

> Acts 4:23
> *"When they had been released, they went to their own companions and reported all that the chief priests and the elders had said to them."*

They are willing to part from their earthly inheritance in order for every one of these "other sons of the father" to be blessed and have all their needs met.

> Acts 2:44-45
> *"And all those who had believed were together and had all things in common; and they began selling their property and possessions and were sharing them with all, as anyone might have need."*

Those who are not connected to the lives of the people within the house in proper covenant relationship, are often the first ones to leave the church in times of adversity. They do not feel strong enough to stand together. God is raising a new community of believers who will be knitted together so that they supply to each other's life and lend strength for each other's achievement.

> Ephesians 4:16
> *"from whom the whole body, being fitted and held together by what every joint supplies, according to the proper working of each individual part, causes the growth of the body for the building up of itself in love."*

E. Sons Must Embrace The Corporate Destiny As The People Of The House

They are a unique company of men and women who have sacrificed their personal agendas and ambitions to pursue the corporate destiny of the whole body. They now believe that in fulfilling the corporate destiny, their own lives will come into the purposes of God. It is obvious that the one who works in the engine room of the ship also reaches the port at the same time as the ship he is labouring in.

They choose to become involved in all that is happening in the house as it will accelerate and quicken each one into God's destiny and direction for their lives. The aspiration of the house becomes the pursuit of the sons. They begin cooperating with each other, labouring together to move forward in Kingdom advancement. They are champions of cooperation rather than champions of competition. They stay tuned to use all their resources and energy to move towards what God is placing upon their hearts. They are there participating at every turn because they are there to pursue the same course and destiny.

> Acts 1:13a
> *"When they had entered the city, they went up to the upper room where they were staying;"*
>
> Acts 1:14
> *"These all with one mind were continually devoting themselves to prayer, along with the women, and Mary the mother of Jesus, and with His brothers."*
>
> Acts 10:24
> *"On the following day he entered Caesarea. Now Cornelius was waiting for them and had called together his relatives and close friends."*

Sons are conscious that they are in this together and will not break ranks when they move forward.

Acts 1:15a
"At this time Peter stood up in the midst of the brethren"

Acts 2:14a
"But Peter, taking his stand with the eleven, raised his voice and declared to them:"

When the sons stand together in purpose and destiny, the people will also recognize that we are standing collectively together. They will know we are a team and that asking one is like asking the whole team!

Acts 2:37
"Now when they heard this, they were pierced to the heart, and said to Peter and the rest of the apostles, "Brethren, what shall we do?""

The church in Antioch responded collectively as one when the Holy Spirit set aside the apostles for the work He has prepared for them outside the local church.

Acts 13:2-3
"While they were ministering to the Lord and fasting, the Holy Spirit said, "Set apart for Me Barnabas and Saul for the work to which I have called them." Then, when they had fasted and prayed and laid their hands on them, they sent them away."

The primary assignment of the church that holds all of us together, brings with it alignment, focus and pursuit of purpose. Energy is not lost and focus is not diverted because we synergize on destiny and are energized by our common goal.

When Jesus commanded the disciples to get into the boat and go to the other side, it was a clear instruction of purpose.

Matthew 14:22
"Immediately He made the disciples get into the boat and go ahead of Him to the other side, while He sent the crowds away."

They got into the boat together and set out under the same instructions. While at sea, the boat was battered by the waves as the winds were contrary. When Jesus came walking on the sea towards them, they became terrified. But Peter, having become certain it was Jesus decided to take action but he moved out of the boat into the sea!

> Matthew 14:28-32
> *"Peter said to Him, "Lord, if it is You, command me to come to You on the water." And He said, "Come!" And Peter got out of the boat, and walked on the water and came toward Jesus. But seeing the wind, he became frightened, and beginning to sink, he cried out, "Lord, save me!" Immediately Jesus stretched out His hand and took hold of him, and *said to him, "You of little faith, why did you doubt?" When they got into the boat, the wind stopped."*

Let's established this fact that it was Jesus' intention and instruction for them to get into the boat and get to the other side. He Himself was coming into the boat while it was being battered by the waves. Peter, however, decided to leave attending to the needs in the boat and moved out of the boat to go to Jesus, even though He was coming toward it. This rationale only belongs to Peter. Whether he was trying to prove that the person coming towards the boat was truly Jesus, or that he merely wanted to experience walking on the water, is a matter of one's own interpretation and opinion. The end result remains that Jesus stretched out His hand and took sinking Peter out of the water and put him back into the boat. Those who are familiar with rearing puppies and kittens would be familiar with the ones who are consistently escaping from the basket and in need of being placed back into it again.

These ones who have a need to explore outside, often disregard the staying together to finish the purpose and assignment which is given. Like Peter, so many would like to move out to gain an experience when our boats are battered by waves and we are in need of their help in the boat. They are out there looking for an adventure and an experience and often at the wrong time. Those who glorify Peter's "great faith" in walking on water must also understand the feelings of others in the boat. This is the gospel according

to those who were left behind in the boat who watched Peter's great faith in action. In fact, while he was sinking, Peter must have had a moment to reflect back on the original instructions of Jesus to stay together in the boat and get to the other side. If we are really honest, Jesus did not mention anything about great faith as so many have assumed.

Sons know how to stay together till the end; until the course is complete and destiny is established.

F. Sons Are Committed To Building The House

Many believers and members enjoy the blessings of the house but do not take the responsibility for the growth of the house. Their mentality is set to receive blessings and receive the best God has for each one of them in each service and meeting. Those who are sons have transited from this mentality and desire to become a blessing to the others in the house. They are willing to rise to their best capacity so that they can provide maximum benefit and blessings to others. They desire to contribute the best with its peak performance so that the others in the house can be greatly blessed. Sons are able to shoulder the responsibility for growth in the house by rising to the occasion to become an answer for the needs or complaints that may arise.

The seven men who were chosen by the people were sufficient to solve the problem permanently and raise the church to the next level.

> Acts 6:6-7
> *"And these they brought before the apostles; and after praying, they laid their hands on them. The word of God kept on spreading; and the number of the disciples continued to increase greatly in Jerusalem, and a great many of the priests were becoming obedient to the faith."*

These sons in the house liberated the apostles from the needs, and accelerated the growth in the body. The word of God kept on spreading into new territories affecting new types of people in the community. Sons can prevent unhealthy practices in the church from stifling the life source in the Set Man and in the appointed leadership of the church. They can become arresters to prevent any distraction and diversion from God's original vision for the house.

G. Sons Feel A Deep Responsibility To Resource The House Regularly

Acts 4:36-37
"Now Joseph, a Levite of Cyprian birth, who was also called Barnabas by the apostles (which translated means Son of Encouragement), and who owned a tract of land, sold it and brought the money and laid it at the apostles' feet."

When we enter a city we are looking for "the son of peace" into whose house we can go and present the gospel of the Kingdom.

Luke 10:6
""If a man of peace is there, your peace will rest on him; but if not, it will return to you."

But when we are raising the church we are looking for "the sons of consolation", like Barnabas, who will stand alongside the Apostles and provide strong support for the move of God in the house. Barnabas represents the type of sons whom God is raising within the house alongside the Set Man. Barnabas had the grace to transit from an old move and reinvent himself to become a model in the fresh move of God. He presents a pattern for our days as we raise sons of consolation within the house.

Firstly, he was willing to leave the old priesthood and enter into a fresh move of God on the earth.

Secondly, he was prepared to be renamed and redefined by the apostles according to the current move of the Holy Spirit. This tantamount to the effects of circumcision that Paul did for Timothy *(Acts 16:3)*. He was willing

to accept a new definition to his identity and person, pursuing a fresh new course.

Thirdly, Barnabas was a son of encouragement to the apostles. He was not just an ordinary exhorter to the believers, but was mature enough to be a blessing to the apostolic men. This armour bearer of the apostles was greatly honoured among the apostles. He found access in relationship with the apostles that allowed him to minister encouragement to the apostles.

Fourthly, he released his resources to accelerate the move of God through the apostles. By laying his resources at their feet he was proclaiming that they prosper in all that God has sent them to do. He affirmed his faith in the direction of God for their lives, and he was participating to honour God's will for them through his sacrifice. The selling of a piece of land by a Levite sends a strong signal that this ex-priest believes in a spiritual inheritance in this future move of God rather than in the past!

Lastly, God positioned this son of encouragement to become the choice instrument to help lead a fresh move of God in Antioch *(Acts 11:22)*. When sons are supporting the fathers in the move of God during the days of their fathers, the sons are positioning themselves to become God's arrows of destiny in their own time and generation. We see that sons are needed to resource their fathers to accelerate the purposes of God in their lives. When the fathers are fast forwarded into the purposes of God, the sons will receive their due reward.

In closing, sonship is God's choice for the House. Not only must we raise up sons of God in the image and likeness of Christ *(Rom 8:29)*, but also raise up honourable men who will be willing to take the legacy of spiritual fathers into new heights.

> 1 Samuel 17:56-58
>
> *"The king said, "You inquire whose son the youth is." So when David returned from killing the Philistine, Abner took him and brought him before Saul with the Philistine's head in his hand. Saul said to him, "Whose son are you, young man?"*

And David answered, "I am the son of your servant Jesse the Bethlehemite.""

People will want to know whose sons we are when we are going into battle. Our success in life is always contributed by many around us especially those who provide the spiritual input and who are stewards of God's grace for us *(Eph 3:2).*

Psalms 127:3-5
"Behold, children are a gift of the LORD, The fruit of the womb is a reward. Like arrows in the hand of a warrior, So are the children of one's youth. How blessed is the man whose quiver is full of them; They will not be ashamed When they speak with their enemies in the gate."

Many pastors are not able to put an end to the enemies' entrance into the city because they are not able to raise up sons in the house. When our quivers are full of arrows (sons in succession available for our assignments) we can then have negotiating power to deal with our enemies. We can keep the enemies outside the gates of the city, not just outside the perimeters of our house. Having sons in the house, increases the spiritual stature of that house and will keep the enemies out of our territories. Raise up sons and they will possess the gates of our enemies.

Genesis 22:17b
"... your seed shall possess the gate of their enemies."

Chapter Eleven

Pastoring The Breakthrough Believers

In *Nehemiah chapter three* we see the orderly restoration of the gates of the city. The first Gate to be restored was the Sheep Gate This reflects the Pastoral Ministry of the Church today. Most of our churches are established strongly on the teaching or evangelistic model, to the neglect of a true shepherding ministry. The "traditional pastoral ministry" is often inclined and founded upon the psychological concepts which exalts the interests of man and downplays the interests of God for the church.

> Matthew 16:23
> *"But He turned and said to Peter, "Get behind Me, Satan! You are a stumbling block to Me; for you are not setting your mind on God's interests, but man's.""*

It is highly centred around man and his needs. Man often takes the centre stage in the affairs and activities of the church forcing the church to exist for him and his welfare. This attitude sums up the humanistic philosophy that has crept into the church. This religious and humanistic pattern traps the Set Man and the people of the house. It would now be virtually impossible to raise a church that will be empowered to do what God has intended her to do because it is so focused on the interests of man. The church is under siege not from devils

but from within. It has been hijacked by those who have come into it with the purpose to stop the work of God from progressing.

> Nehemiah 4:11
> *"Our enemies said, "They will not know or see until we come among them, kill them and put a stop to the work.""*

Satanic infiltration into the activities of the church is inevitable when she becomes focused only on the interests of man. Humanistic thought patterns, procedures and human traditions invalidate the word of God. The Pharisees were experts at setting aside God's commandments in order to keep their own traditions. They taught as doctrines the percepts of men, and their interpretation of the laws of God overshadowed the spirit of truth and all that God wanted. They oppressed the next generation with their creed and secured their own positions of authority over the people.

> Mark 7:7-9
> *"'BUT IN VAIN DO THEY WORSHIP ME, TEACHING AS DOCTRINES THE PRECEPTS OF MEN.' "Neglecting the commandment of God, you hold to the tradition of men." He was also saying to them, "You are experts at setting aside the commandment of God in order to keep your tradition."*

> Mark 7:13
> *"thus invalidating the word of God by your tradition which you have handed down; and you do many things such as that.""*

When we raise the standard of God and bring back accurate apostolic patterns of behaviour and belief systems, false prophets and false teachers will be exposed *(Mark 7:3-5)*. A new generation operating and modelling a new frequency of truth will expose an inaccurate generation before it. It will further expose the inaccurate interpretations of their teachers and instructors.

God is restoring the apostolic teaching ministry that will bring back true order and government to His house. One of the first areas of government is in the area of the Pastoral Ministry of the church.

Redefining The Pastoral Ministry

Proverbs 27:23-24

"Know well the condition of your flocks, And pay attention to your herds; For riches are not forever, Nor does a crown endure to all generations."

The Pastor is exhorted to know well the condition and spiritual state of his flock. He is to have a radical review of the health of his church not just the numerical growth of his church. Most pastors gauge their success by the "numbers in attendance" and the "figures in collections". Their "facts and figures approach" is the beginning of a corrupt priesthood. Essentially most pastors consider the above as church growth without realizing that their concept will be counted unproductive in the future. This perspective will drive the church to be established around the thinking patterns of the secular corporation. Most mega churches are implementing these structures of management which will cause them to become barren in their process to reproduce the next generation of sons for accurate succession.

The Pastor must know well the actual state of the people whom God has entrusted to him. As the Teacher presents himself approved to God as a workman who need not be ashamed accurately handling the word of truth *(2 Tim 2:15)*, the Pastor must accurately handle the flock of God. He has to pay attention to them as all his life, ministry and resources are going to be shaped by the flock.

The Pastor's personal resources and riches are not going to last forever but his people are going to continue into the next generation. Thus if they become his rich assets and generous provision, he will be blessed all the days of his life. The Pastor's crown or rule and authority does not endure or continue to every generation but if the people are connected and fathered, his legacy will be the primary source of blessing to the generations to come.

It is often said that the people are the church's greatest asset. More accurately it should read as, "the right people are church's greatest asset". We all know to our sorrow what the wrong people or "wronged" people can do to a church.

The Pastor must pay attention to the PEOPLE as this is his field of expertise. His future is tied up to his people. His legacy is going to be transferred to his people. Thus he must pay attention to those with him and around him in leadership as well as those below him in membership.

> Proverbs 27:25
> *"When the grass disappears, the new growth is seen, And the herbs of the mountains are gathered in,"*

The Pastor must know when the seasons of God change in his church, he must do the appropriate things needed in his ministry to the people. When the grass in the fields disappears he must have hay in the barn stored up for them. When the new growth of fresh grass breaks out he must move his flock out from the barn to graze in the fields. The shepherd must also gather the herbs from the mountains to provide added nourishment to the flock. The flock will not know what herbs are good and what are bad for them. He is the one who provides the added ingredients for their wellbeing. The Pastoral ministry is so essential for the wellbeing and for the health of the church.

> Proverbs 27:26-27
> *"The lambs will be for your clothing, And the goats will bring the price of a field, And there will be goats' milk enough for your food, For the food of your household, And sustenance for your maidens."*

The Pastoral Ministry that is effective will be well cared for and provided for. There will be no financial lack or lack of personnel or manpower. The flock will be the reason for the abundant provision in the house. There will be food, clothing and needed sustenance for the whole household. Another interesting factor is; the mortgage on the field that the shepherd has incurred is covered or paid back by the produce of the flock. The allowance and maintenance of all our fellow workers in ministry *(maidens v. 27)* will be covered and met. Whatever it cost to raise a

strong local church full of godly people will be offset and covered by the resources we will discover within the house. It will pay off at the end. Pastors, we need to know well the condition of the flock and so pay attention to the herd!

The Pastoral Requirements Of Sheep

There are seven major needs related to the sheep that clarifies the requirements for accurate Pastoral Ministry today. Compromising these needs will cause an imbalance to take place in the house of God. The wisdom found in these pages is peaceable, as it will remove stress of mind and heart in the Pastor. The wisdom of God is the signature anointing of an accurate ministry as it will help the Pastor build the House of God.

James 3:17-18
"But the wisdom from above is first pure, then peaceable, gentle, reasonable, full of mercy and good fruits, unwavering, without hypocrisy. And the seed whose fruit is righteousness is sown in peace by those who make peace."

A. The Sheep Must Have Their Needs Met

Psalms 23:1
"The LORD is my shepherd, I shall not want."

The Pastoral Ministry must first meet the needs of the people effectively and efficiently. The felt needs must be met so that it does not hinder the spiritual progress of the believers. The ability to change their state by destroying what is limiting and affecting them from moving forward in Kingdom advancement is essential for every pastor.

Acts 2:40
"And with many other words he solemnly testified and kept on exhorting them, saying, "Be saved from this perverse generation!""

The Pastoral Ministry must first exercise the authority to cut off and bind every influence, every vehicle of corruption and every oppression on the believers. We must deliver them from out of the domain of darkness so that they are now added to the Kingdom of God.

Colossians 1:13
"For He rescued us from the domain of darkness, and transferred us to the kingdom of His beloved Son,"

Acts 2:41
"So then, those who had received his word were baptized; and that day there were added about three thousand souls."

A disturbed sheep will create frustration to the whole herd. One restless sheep can create a vulnerable situation for the whole company. One can cause many to become defiled!

Hebrews 12:15
"See to it that no one comes short of the grace of God; that no root of bitterness springing up causes trouble, and by it many be defiled;"

B. The Sheep Needs Healthy Food To Grow In Stature

Matthew 24:24
""For false Christs and false prophets will arise and will show great signs and wonders, so as to mislead, if possible, even the elect."

A very important requirement in the Pastoral Ministry is the ability to discern what type of food is needed and who needs it the most. The sheep need to be fed with the word of God at the proper time.

The "baby" must be given the "water" of the Word which is the "foundational aspects" of Kingdom life *(Eph 5:26)*. He now has the "knowledge of salvation" and he is born again.

The "infant" is given the "milk" of the Word which is the "devotional aspects" of Kingdom life *(Heb 5:13, 1 Cor 3:2-3)*. He now enjoys the "effects of salvation" and he is blessed.

The "young man" is given the "meat" of the Word which is the "eternal purposes of God" for his Kingdom life *(Jn 4:34, 5:30, 36)*. He is beginning to realize the "Purpose of Salvation" is more than just being blessed but he needs to become a blessing by serving God's Purposes *(Phil 3:12-13)*.

The "father" is given "solid food" of the Word which is the "Wisdom to Mature" *(1 Cor 2:6-8, 13, 16)*. He is beginning to realize that "Maturity to Manhood through Salvation" is an ongoing experience that is needed. This allows him to find stature in God.

The "mature fathers" are given "Hidden Manna" of the Word which is the "Fellowship with the Father". He is beginning to know the "Counsel of the Lord and His Proceeding Word". He is now becoming God's representative here on the earth.

Feeding is often wrongly associated with the teaching ministry. Teaching is not feeding as we can teach our children algebra and not be feeding them anything! Teaching is educating them and changing their thinking patterns. This knowledge transfer helps them change their behaviour patterns and become mature in character and expression of kingdom lifestyle. Feeding restores the whole person by working out salvation from within. It is an internal growth of the spirit man in wholeness. Our feeding gives nourishment to the inner man and helps his inner man rise to maturity. A child can have lots of computer lessons and piano classes and be physically under-nourished. The Pastoral Ministry needs to develop the ability to feed the flock with good pasture *(Jn 10:9)*.

The ability to grow each believer into maturity of manhood is often a neglected part of the Pastoral Ministry. We are entrenched into a strong teaching ministry dispensing knowledge and information. The state of the flock does not change even though they now look intelligent and knowledgeable. Those who are being fed accurately will mature in manhood and in discernment. They will not be

vulnerable or gullible. They will not be tossed to and fro by every wind of the doctrines of man.

Ephesians 4:14-16

"As a result, we are no longer to be children, tossed here and there by waves and carried about by every wind of doctrine, by the trickery of men, by craftiness in deceitful scheming; but speaking the truth in love, we are to grow up in all aspects into Him who is the head, even Christ, from whom the whole body, being fitted and held together by what every joint supplies, according to the proper working of each individual part, causes the growth of the body for the building up of itself in love."

C. The Sheep Needs To Be Cared For And Loved

One of the most wholesome anointings is the relational grace of the shepherding ministry. The care and love that is released from the heart of true shepherds has a healing grace to bring restoration on the souls of men.

Psalms 23:2-3

"He makes me lie down in green pastures; He leads me beside quiet waters. He restores my soul; He guides me in the paths of righteousness For His name's sake."

The Hand of God is not only one of authority but also of care and love. He leads us by streams of living waters and restores our souls. This ministry's grace provides the healing balm over the afflictions of the soul. When the soul of a righteous man is oppressed he can become weary and frustrated. It can lead him into inaccurate ways of behaviour and he may put forth his hands to do wrong.

The shepherds have an ability to guide them into the path of righteousness even during difficult times like this. The shepherd's love and care for them can see them through. This reassuring love of the Shepherd and the under shepherd can empower us to rise above the fear of death and the evil works of the enemy.

D. The Sheep Needs A Strong Leader

John 10:3-4
""... and he calls his own sheep by name and leads them out. When he puts forth all his own, he goes ahead of them, and the sheep follow him because they know his voice."

The Pastoral Ministry is established by a strong leadership grace. We cannot work on suggestion and democracy. We are the under shepherds of the Great Shepherd who purchased them by His own blood. The sheep will be at risk if we allow them to go astray *(Is 53:6)*. There is an enemy who is constantly prowling around for someone to devour. As Pastors, we are to lead them into safety and protect them from danger when they are vulnerable.

John 10:11-13
""I am the good shepherd; the good shepherd lays down His life for the sheep. "He who is a hired hand, and not a shepherd, who is not the owner of the sheep, sees the wolf coming, and leaves the sheep and flees, and the wolf snatches them and scatters them. "He flees because he is a hired hand and is not concerned about the sheep."

The emphasis of the Pastoral Ministry today of just loveing and caring for the flock is allowing the enemy to take advantage of the sheep that are straying. When Pastoral Ministries provide strong leadership we can take the sheep beyond their fears because "our rod and our staff" can comfort them. The leadership of the shepherd can take them through the valley of the shadow of death and our sheep can be secure in the midst of all the evil around them. The true shepherds can even prepare a banqueting table for them in the presence of their enemies. None of these things will cause them to fear or be intimidated because of the strength of leadership provided by the Pastors who are leading them.

Psalms 23:4-5

"Even though I walk through the valley of the shadow of death, I fear no evil, for You are with me; Your rod and Your staff, they comfort me. You prepare a table before me in the presence of my enemies; You have anointed my head with oil; My cup overflows."

Most Pastors do not take a strong leadership for fear of being seen as dictatorial. This misconception has allowed the enemy to prey upon the church. The humanistic thought pattern of allowing believers to decide for themselves is dangerous if we have not taught them accurate government. Allowing someone make his own decision without first raising them into maturity that can help them decide accurately, is due to the lack of understanding of Kingdom principles. We must not just teach people the power of the freedom of choice, but also the power of government and how good government in our lives bring peace, prosperity and stability. We must choose good government and we can exercise our freedom of choice under the atmosphere of safety and security. We must choose good government not just the freedom of choice!

Good leaders train the church to subject themselves to good government and delegated authority. This freedom to give up our rights and subject ourselves to accurate government is essential. It is by being subjected to one another that we bring the kingdom community lifestyle into existence. By yielding our will and choosing to submit under God's appointed spiritual authority we can be saved and live securely. True pastoral ministries will impress upon the people the need to stay under authority and thus under protection and covering.

E. The Sheep Need To Be Trained To Hear His Voice

The Pastoral Ministry must carry the word of the Spirit and the Spirit of counsel in their mouth continually so that the people will become trained to hear God's voice consistently.

1 Thessalonians 2:13
"For this reason we also constantly thank God that when you received the word of God which you heard from us, you accepted it not as the word of men, but for what it really is, the word of God, which also performs its work in you who believe."

John 10:27
""My sheep hear My voice, and I know them, and they follow Me;"

The leadership of the church needs to become the mouthpiece of God before the sheep. In hearing their voice the members must become sensitive to God's voice. When the local shepherd speaks, the voice of the True Shepherd must be heard. By hearing our voices the sheep becomes accustomed to the frequencies of the Holy Spirit.

Matthew 11:16-17
""But to what shall I compare this generation? It is like children sitting in the market places, who call out to the other children, and say, 'We played the flute for you, and you did not dance; we sang a dirge, and you did not mourn.'"

This wicked generation can be compared to a generation of people who are impaired from receiving the frequency of heaven. There is confusion in every street and other voices are clamouring to invade our attention.

Proverbs 1:20-21
"Wisdom shouts in the street, She lifts her voice in the square; At the head of the noisy streets she cries out; At the entrance of the gates in the city she utters her sayings:"

God's voice must not be drowned in the Marketplace. We must find strategic positions in society and in the House of God to bring God's wisdom to the right people. We must bring God's word and voice to become the foundation and centre stage for all our activities. People are constantly standing at the head of every street asking the questions of where it is leading. Those at the entrance of the gates in the city must have within them the power to

help decide the course of action that will save and protect the whole city. Without the voice of God going out, the naive ones will not find discernment and the simple minded, the accurate course of action.

John 10:5
""A stranger they simply will not follow, but will flee from him, because they do not know the voice of strangers.""

The Shepherd's voice becomes the plum bline to discern the voice of the strangers. The Pastoral Ministry must carry the frequency of the Great Shepherd's voice. This will cause those who hear them to become familiar and tuned to the frequency of His Voice.

1 Corinthians 2:1
"And when I came to you, brethren, I did not come with superiority of speech or of wisdom, proclaiming to you the testimony of God."

When the Apostle Paul came to the Corinthian church he came proclaiming the testimony of God to them. He was declaring what God was saying about them so that their faith could now rest on the power of God. Paul calls this type of communication as speaking the wisdom of God.

1 Corinthians 2:6
"Yet we do speak wisdom among those who are mature; a wisdom, however, not of this age nor of the rulers of this age, who are passing away;"

This dimension of communication will allow the church to come into the knowledge of all that God has prepared for those who love Him. This type of training will bring the church into maturity as they become taught by the Spirit.

1 Corinthians 2:13
"which things we also speak, not in words taught by human wisdom, but in those taught by the Spirit, combining spiritual thoughts with spiritual words."

The Pastoral Ministry must combine spiritual thoughts with spirit words and release these things of the Spirit to the people. Those who are adequately trained will be able to access these revelations and will be able to understand them *(1 Cor 2:14-16).* This flow of revelation will renew their minds and cause their minds to become tuned to the frequencies of the mind of Christ. With accurate Pastoral input, the minds of the members will become renewed and they will be able to yield to the mind of the Lord. As the Son worked with the Father the believers can now walk into sonship and be led by the Holy Spirit. This is one of the most powerful influences of the Pastoral Ministry!

F. The Sheep Can Enter Through The Door The Shepherd Opens

The Pastoral Ministry can bring the sheep into greater heights of experiences in God. This aspect of the ministerial responsibilities is often neglected due to inaccurate understanding of the Pastoral role functions. The Shepherd is the door through which the sheep pass through and find pasture.

> John 10:9
> *""I am the door; if anyone enters through Me, he will be saved, and will go in and out and find pasture."*

The Pastoral Ministry has a tremendous responsibility to breakthrough for their people by opening pathways in the spirit. These breakthroughs the Pastors have personally experienced and pioneered into, will set the precedence for their members. We set an example for others to follow. We are able to show the way out of the oppression and we can chart the course of true victory for others by modelling it in our lives. This encourages the people as they will believe when we are able to reveal the procedure towards the achievement of true victory. As leaders we can open up new areas of breakthrough for the church members.

> Acts 11:20-21
> *"But there were some of them, men of Cyprus and Cyrene, who came to Antioch and began speaking to the Greeks also, preaching the Lord Jesus. And the hand of the Lord was with them, and a large number who believed turned to the Lord."*

It is always the "some of them" who open the pathway of the spirit for the "rest of them"!

The Pastoral Ministry has the ability and the leadership grace to lead the sheep into different dimensions of life and growth. The Shepherd not only leads the sheep beside quiet waters, but also through the valley of the shadow of death. It is also the shepherd's grace to anoint the head of the sheep with oil so that the presence of the enemy will not cause them to become vulnerable. Their ability to stay under the leadership grace of the Shepherd and partake what is provided, protects them from demonic attacks.

> Psalms 23:2, 4-5
> *"He makes me lie down in green pastures; He leads me beside quiet waters. ... Even though I walk through the valley of the shadow of death, I fear no evil, for You are with me; Your rod and Your staff, they comfort me. You prepare a table before me in the presence of my enemies; You have anointed my head with oil; My cup overflows."*

The Pastoral grace of the true Shepherd can cause the believers to find an abundant life until their cup overflows. They can experience goodness and lovingkindness all the days of their lives. These believers can come into such a dimension of life, as they have found a place of belonging in the House of God and a place of involvement with God and all what He is doing in that church and city!

What an amazing grace to open up for every member of His House. We need to guide all of those in God's flock who are in the various fields of expertise, and bring them into their place of operation in and through the House. The Pastoral leadership must find this grace to open up life, and life abundantly for the members of the House. This is God's call upon those who are His under shepherds and those who chose to represent Him accurately.

> John 10:10b
> *"... I came that they may have life, and have it abundantly."*

G. The Sheep Must Know The Other Sheep That Belong To The Shepherd

This is a dimension of the Pastoral Ministry that is often neglected. We must teach the individual members in the church to recognize the other sheep who are connected to us as shepherds. The believers must connect with others in their midst who are also connecting with the Pastor in the same way they do. They must recognize their father's other sons and relate with them as with their brothers. We relate not just because we know them personally and intimately. We relate initially because they are part of our family. This is the simple basis for starting to care and share. The power of the believers lies in the synergy of the community. By the meaningful aspects of sharing, caring and coordinating with one another, the strength of the church is enhanced. Most people are champions of competition and not of cooperation, thus they cause the corporate grace to become depleted. This lack of integration and interaction can cause the corporate anointing to become frustrated.

The Pastoral Ministry must be able to bring the believers into a deep sense of belonging to the House and to the family of God. The believers must be able to feel an intense passion to belong to the Kingdom community. Their attitude towards the House and all those who choose this extended family must be positive.

> Acts 2:44-47
> *"And all those who had believed were together and had all things in common; and they began selling their property and possessions and were sharing them with all, as anyone might have need. Day by day continuing with one mind in the temple, and breaking bread from house to house, they were taking their meals together with gladness and sincerity of heart, praising God and having favor with all the people. And the Lord was adding to their number day by day those who were being saved."*

In *Acts 2* Their desire to be together and share their lives gave them a corporate identity. They not only did it as a discipline, but for the love of

coming together as a family. They celebrated it with meals and thanksgiving. The Lord was adding to their members, day by day those who are being saved. It is difficult to be added to the number of those who are miserable and contentious. We feel more welcome in a happy crowd than in the midst of a volatile crowd!

The Pastoral Ministry provides a unique grace that will cause believers to share life and resources together. This Kingdom community becomes an alternative lifestyle to the old religious lifestyle they have had in the past. This newfound family celebrates each other's presence. They choose to be a blessing one to another. They are happy to meet, but their meeting goes beyond the context of a religious belief. They saw the reality of a new holy nation and a royal priesthood. The church becomes the kingdom community, the gathering point for those who chose to believe in Jesus. Everyone who believed in the Lord Jesus became part of this kingdom community.

The Pastoral Ministry will bring the sheep into the fold and every new one added to it will find their place and their function.

> Romans 12:5
> *"so we, who are many, are one body in Christ, and individually members one of another."*
>
> 1 Corinthians 12:20
> *"But now there are many members, but one body."*
>
> 1 Corinthians 12:24b, 25-27
> *"... But God has so composed the body, giving more abundant honor to that member which lacked, so that there may be no division in the body, but that the members may have the same care for one another. And if one member suffers, all the members suffer with it; if one member is honored, all the members rejoice with it. Now you are Christ's body, and individually members of it."*

Chapter Twelve

Boundaries Of Responsibilities Of Breakthrough Believers

The unrealistic expectations and demands placed upon the Pastoral Ministry can weigh the Pastors down and discourage them. Often these expectations are painfully misplaced. Those who are attending the church may not feel the same intensity of passion for the work as the Set Man of the house. The Set Man could be going on an overdrive and giving out more than a hundred percent of himself for the work, but a believer coming to his church may not feel the same. He may be there because the church is conveniently situated relative to his home, or because the services are starting later in the morning than the other church he used to attend. A person added under this lack of value of perspective, will eventually move out into a more convenient place when the church he is currently attending makes any changes which create an inconvenience or discomfort to his "same zone" mentality.

The Pastor must discern those whom he is receiving from the Lord and those who are being "added" to their number. Many could be attending the meetings regularly but yet, operate on a different frequency to what the Pastor is feeling. When we are clear of whom the Lord is adding, we can expect the best from them and not be disappointed.

We must know whom the Lord is adding to the number. I once saw a vision of a man gathering fruits from the branch of a large tree that was inclining into his backyard. He was so thrilled that he was having such an abundant harvest in his backyard. The actual tree was about twenty or thirty feet away and was rooted in the neighbouring compound. So many pastors are having an inclining and fruitful branch of another man's tree in their compound without realizing that the roots of the tree is in another man's ground. We could be eating the fruits and enjoying the benefits of another man's labour, but remember this, people will always go back to where their roots are.

For this reason so many Charismatic churches have people in their midst with different roots, and that is why they would now need to please everyone so that none will leave. They are still stuck in their own denominational mentality even though they are physically present in our backyard. Their roots are not in our ground. They do not stand where we stand on most issues, but we accommodate them. We have the "different strokes for different folks," theory!

The same problems were experienced during the Charismatic days. The denominational churches were losing members to the independent Charismatic churches. They decided to open up other additional services while the other remained traditional. Instead of losing the members, they accommodated them and gave them what they wanted. They were seen as being "tolerant" and open to the move of God. Little, in fact, did change in most of these churches. Those who stayed within the institutional churches fossilized!

Today, we do the same and we have many honourable words to describe our actions. We clothe our actions with more prestigious terminology and quote the more notable ministry names to validate our actions. How wise can a foolish man be? We cannot be doing the same thing, the same way and expect different results! The type of people that remain within our church will ultimately determine the nature of ministry in the future. Thus attracting the wrong crowd today and feeding their frenzy, will mean that we have sealed our own future by our present choices. We have determined within our own hearts and revealed our stand for what actually dwells in our hearts.

The choices we make in compromising to keep this crowd by playing to the

gallery will be profitable for the now. The crowd remains with the church and with the resources and does not leave the territory. We have prevented the "exodus" and we desire to keep them for the future. Most Pastors foresight ends here!

The "bones of Joseph" will be prophesying of God's purposes for the people of Israel in Egypt. These stirrings will rise up in the next generations as God moves closer to fulfilling these proceeding words from heaven.

> Acts 7:17
> *""But as the time of the promise was approaching which God had assured to Abraham, the people increased and multiplied in Egypt,"*

God will engineer the circumstances for change and usher in a new move within the church. This is where churches fail. They have become so structured and conditioned that they have become fossilized and institutionalized! The temptation to grow a sizable church, compromising the future for the present, is very high among Pastors.

The key to avoid this disaster is to grow the right type of people consistently and purposefully. It is the people factor that will determine our future achievements. The church must always have this breed of breakthrough believers. A new breed without greed, a radical opposition to greed, corruption and religious devils! We are not guilty of the temptations of compromise because we use different bait for different fish, but because of what we make out of the people we bring into the church.

> Matthew 23:15
> *""Woe to you, scribes and Pharisees, hypocrites, because you travel around on sea and land to make one proselyte; and when he becomes one, you make him twice as much a son of hell as yourselves."*

If the church gathers the people for "attendance" and "an offering" instead of bringing them into maturity so that they can fulfil corporate destiny in that city

and nation, we are doomed to repeat the error of the past. The *twenty third chapter* of *Matthew* reveals to us why Jesus was heavy on the Pharisees. The Pharisees used the people to consolidate their own position and propagate their traditions. They kept the people in an oppressed state. The people were distressed and dispirited like sheep without a shepherd. The Pharisees brought the people into a religious system which gave them authority to oppress whosoever they wanted. Jesus hates this religious order which through His death He made obsolete.

> Hebrews 8:13
> *"When He said, "A new covenant," He has made the first obsolete. But whatever is becoming obsolete and growing old is ready to disappear."*

The danger of raising a whole Priesthood and style of ministry that has already been rejected is our present cause for concern. We need to yield to the Order of Melchizedek which perfects the believer and pushes him forward into the maturity of sonship.

> Hebrews 10:1-2
> *"For the Law, since it has only a shadow of the good things to come and not the very form of things, can never, by the same sacrifices which they offer continually year by year, make perfect those who draw near. Otherwise, would they not have ceased to be offered, because the worshipers, having once been cleansed, would no longer have had consciousness of sins?"*

> Hebrews 10:19-21
> *"Therefore, brethren, since we have confidence to enter the holy place by the blood of Jesus, by a new and living way which He inaugurated for us through the veil, that is, His flesh, and since we have a great priest over the house of God,"*

The immediate need of the ministry is to find a way of raising the people into the maturity of manhood as sons. We need to bring the Body into her proper working condition so that she is able to fulfil the eternal purpose which God brought about in Christ.

Ephesians 3:10-11
"so that the manifold wisdom of God might now be made known through the church to the rulers and the authorities in the heavenly places. This was in accordance with the eternal purpose which He carried out in Christ Jesus our Lord,"

Ephesians 4:13
"until we all attain to the unity of the faith, and of the knowledge of the Son of God, to a mature man, to the measure of the stature which belongs to the fullness of Christ."

Identifying And Responding To The People Groups In The City

There are seven types of people groups in the city and understanding these groups of people and their perspectives will allow the Pastor to respond accurately. The Pastor can learn to relate and respond wisely to each of these people groups. This will allow him to avoid disappointment, false expectations and false hopes. He can then employ the right strategy to reach and work with them. Each type of fish is lured by different bait and for each category of people we need to use a different approach and means to influence and impact them.

After we have brought them to the knowledge of the benefits of salvation we must mature them into the purposes of salvation. We must help them transit into kingdom mentality and bring them into a place of sonship in the house to extend the kingdom of God.

The Pastoral aspect of the church will handle five of these groups which are already within the church, while the first two must be worked on through the evangelistic thrust. Though we need the prophetic, teaching and apostolic mantles for an accurate building of a governing church, these two graces (pastoral and evangelistic) are dominant in shaping the people in these two people groups.

A. The Community Or Society

This category of people are those who live in our society and in our city. They are the general public that have not come into a meaningful contact with the church. They do not know us as we have not yet broken into their world. However, they are aware of our presence and our activities as a church. They are our mission field and the pool of our future members. This is considered as our fishing pond. Every member of the Community must be viewed as a potential member of our church if we could give each one of them an opportunity to make a personal decision to follow Christ.

B. The Crowds

These people in our community are not only aware of our presence and activities as a church, but they have already found bridges and common grounds to connect meaningfully with us. They have come in contact with friends or close relatives who are part of the church. They have come into the services and functions organized by the local church. Their attendance at our functions signals their support for our cause. Unfortunately, these people have not given themselves to become part of the church life and membership. Though they only support our cause at their convenience, we should maintain a cordial relationship with them. Though these sympathizers do not want to identify with us, we need to keep the bridges open with a strong friendship factor and thrust.

C. The Congregation

The congregation includes all those who are believers and who attend our services regularly as potential members as well as committed members. The fringe category of the congregation are not involved in any responsibility for the growth or maintenance of the church. They are loosely attached to the House. They have chosen to fellowship with us and identify with the church as their home and place of worship. They are there because their needs are met. They have come to be blessed, but they do not have a specific desire or lack thereof to build with us. They are merely faithful to our programs as it benefits them. Though these are our spiritual members they have yet to develop a mentality to build the church together with us. They have not come into the flow of body life.

> Ephesians 4:16
> *"from whom the whole body, being fitted and held together by what every joint supplies, according to the proper working of each individual part, causes the growth of the body for the building up of itself in love."*

D. The Committed Members

These are members of the church who have been integrated into the life stream of the church. They identify with the lifestyle and in the practice of kingdom purposes in the church. They have come to interact with one another and have employed their skills and gifts and resources to serve one another. These have become functioning members. They have learned to work in submission to God's appointed and delegated leadership authority. They have learnt to work for a collective goal and vision. Their desire for active involvement keeps the church healthy and functional. These have matured in kingdom living and have become weaned from self-centredness. We can survive as a church without any involvement of the fringe members but without committed members the church does not exist and will cease to function.

E. The Core Members

These are the inner circle membership who are directly involved in working with and supporting the leadership of the local house. These are the armour bearers of the leadership and the church can be built around those who are well connected to the main pillars. These core members are visibly involved with leadership and they can efficiently carry the weight of the work on their

own shoulders. They are taking kingdom responsibility and are in training for accurate leadership in the future. They are trainable materials for future leadership roles. These core members have been proven trustworthy and are being trained and prepared for promotion into different levels of leadership. Blessed is the pastor who has a great quantity of committed members and core members for he shall have a great supply of labourers to bring in the harvest.

F. The Co-Labourers

These are the fellow workers and fellow soldiers together with the Senior Pastor. These are the Leadership Team covering the maintenance, administrative and pastoral ministry. These are all our structural leaders who are directly involved with the Set Man in bringing government to the House. They are the main pillars with leadership roles that represent fully the spirit and heart of the father of the house. The Pastoral oversight acts as pastoral elders to provide spiritual input into the church. They exercise decision-making authority to help the church move forward in Kingdom advancement. They help to implement the vision of the house. They are the bridge between the father of the house and the committed people of the house. Co-labourers have some measure of executive powers to bring about the implementation of the vision and strategies of the Set Man. These co-labourers, being main pillars, are set on the same course as the Set Man to fulfil destiny together. They form the inner circle of trusted ones worthy of succession.

G. The Council

The Council is the "circle within the circle" or "wheel within the wheel". Though the four and twenty elders were around the throne, the four cherubim were set around the immediate vicinity of the throne.

> Revelations 4:9-10
> *"And when the living creatures give glory and honor and thanks to Him who sits on the throne, to Him who lives forever and ever,*

the twenty-four elders will fall down before Him who sits on the throne, and will worship Him who lives forever and ever, and will cast their crowns before the throne, saying,"

This company of leaders are elders of the house who are specifically involved in providing clarity to the purpose and direction of the church. They are responsible to capture and articulate the visions of God for this house they represent. They receive that mandate from heaven and are God's prophetic voice to the company of believers they represent and lead.

In a pioneering work the Pastor and his wife play this role and are committed with this responsibility. As the work grows both numerically and spiritually, others who are standing in succession will have the opportunity to reveal what they are carrying in their spirits. The Council must become one voice, one team and represent the purpose and destiny of God has for the church. They must know in depth what God is requiring of this church and where He is leading it. The Council must have such a unity of the Spirit as well as unity of the faith to labour as one. The unity of the Spirit comes out of the Holy Spirit uniting us under His direction and inspiration. However, the unity of the faith deals with the courage and convictions of the Holy Spirit in our hearts that help us synergize together in our collective pursuit of the purposes of God towards the destiny He has set for us. The unity of faith means we have received the same insight and understanding of the proceeding word and we agree on a certain course of action to bring implementation of what we have received. We will walk together until His will is done on earth as it is in heaven. It is more difficult to find a Council than a Committee. A Council carries the Mind and Counsels of the Purposes of God whereas a committee is the administrative arm to bring execution and implementation to what has already been decided. A committee can help the administration of a project but a Council embraces and gives birth to what God is releasing on the earth.

Isaiah 6:8
"Then I heard the voice of the Lord, saying, "Whom shall I send, and who will go for Us?" Then I said, "Here am I. Send me!""

It takes time and a thorough cleansing process to raise a Council. We cannot be yoked to the people and carry their burden and still hope to effectively represent God to them. We must be re-commissioned like Isaiah and become the representative of Heaven and God. The Council members are His mouthpiece and His representative towards the people. They speak for Him and are available to show Him forth.

The Practical Responsibilities Of Breakthrough Believers

A. Pursuing The Mission Purpose Of The Church

Every member is responsible to pusue the Mission Purpose of the house. The "mission statement of purpose" describes our reason for existence and our direction into the future. It does not change every year as it describes our unchangeable destiny. The "vision statement of strategy" describes how we are going to get there and how the administration and implementation of this mission is going to be.

The members in the House pursue this collective corporate destiny that God has for all of us together. The members are totally committed to the course the church is taking. They are there to give their full and strong support to move together towards what God requires of us. The members must know that they have joined a House that is going towards what God has commissioned us towards. Their joining to the House as they are "added to their company" must not hijack the purpose of God for her. They must not divert her attention and strength from fulfilling His will. Neither will they distract her from moving towards God's purposes by overwhelming her with their needs and inadequacies. They are there to be a blessing to her and inspire her to finish the course.

Acts 6:2-4

"So the twelve summoned the congregation of the disciples and said, "It is not desirable for us to neglect the word of God in order to serve tables. "Therefore, brethren, select from among you seven men of good reputation, full of the Spirit and of wisdom, whom we may put in charge of this task. "But we will devote ourselves to prayer and to the ministry of the word.""

B. Applying The Proceeding Word Into Daily Living

Hebrews 5:12

"For though by this time you ought to be teachers, you have need again for someone to teach you the elementary principles of the oracles of God, and you have come to need milk and not solid food."

Hebrews 3:12-13, 15

"Take care, brethren, that there not be in any one of you an evil, unbelieving heart that falls away from the living God. But encourage one another day after day, as long as it is still called "Today," so that none of you will be hardened by the deceitfulness of sin. ... while it is said, "TODAY IF YOU HEAR HIS VOICE, DO NOT HARDEN YOUR HEARTS, AS WHEN THEY PROVOKED ME.""

Hebrews 4:7

"He again fixes a certain day, "Today," saying through David after so long a time just as has been said before, "TODAY IF YOU HEAR HIS VOICE, DO NOT HARDEN YOUR HEARTS.""

Every member is responsible understand and receive insight into applying the proceeding word of God for the season into their daily life. Every member of the governing church must be attentive to what the Holy Spirit is saying to the church. The present word will produce faith in our spirit and cause us to take on the wisdom of God for its accurate implementation so that we can build on an accurate lifestyle.

Matthew 7:24

""Therefore everyone who hears these words of Mine and acts on them, may be compared to a wise man who built his house on the rock."

We need to raise up a new generation that will hear God's word and mix it with faith, so that they can enter into the rest of God. Their faith and obedience will cause them to cease from their own labours and allow God to display His works among them.

Hebrews 4:2

"For indeed we have had good news preached to us, just as they also; but the word they heard did not profit them, because it was not united by faith in those who heard."

The emphasis of the church should be obedience and becoming doers of the word and not just being hearers only. This is the cognitive curse currently choking the church from true spiritual growth. The people have learnt the deceptive habit of agreeing with the preacher and responding to his eloquence and dynamics in the services, but to the total neglect of obedience to the word after the services are over. We have raised an entire generation of believers who enjoy the word and its revelation, but who are not living examples of the message they have heard. Though Herod enjoyed the preaching of John, he never gave heed to what he heard from John.

Mark 6:20

"for Herod was afraid of John, knowing that he was a righteous and holy man, and he kept him safe. And when he heard him, he was very perplexed; but he used to enjoy listening to him."

The emphasis of explicit obedience to His word must return to the House of God and we will then see the miraculous acts of God in demonstration.

It is those who can bring the members into a devoted lifestyle to accurate teaching who will also lead the way to harvest of the miraculous and the demonstration of the manifested Presence of God.

Acts 2:42-43

"They were continually devoting themselves to the apostles' teaching and to fellowship, to the breaking of bread and to prayer. Everyone kept feeling a sense of awe; and many wonders and signs were taking place through the apostles."

C. Own Spiritual Development And Growth

Every member is responsible for the development and growth of his own life spiritually. The pastoral ministry is not a social work of looking after retarded spiritual babies who cannot do what they should be doing for themselves. Neither is it a ministry to baby-sit those who would not take responsibility to grow up in order to shoulder the burden of the work of building His House. We can bring the horse to the water but we cannot force it to drink. We observe the immaturity of the believers across the Body of Christ who choose to stay in their state and refuse to do anything for themselves. Religion has "fried their brains and have frozen their wills in a particular way of operation that will keep them in the cycle of defeat."

John 5:5-7

*"A man was there who had been ill for thirty-eight years. When Jesus saw him lying there, and knew that he had already been a long time in that condition, He *said to him, "Do you wish to get well?" The sick man answered Him, "Sir, I have no man to put me into the pool when the water is stirred up, but while I am coming, another steps down before me.""*

Only religious folks will sit around in one place for thirty eight years without trying anything new. They are still waiting for "someone" to help them into the pool. Religion has shut this man in its grip so much that Jesus had to come into its territory and get the man out. We must press into our own breakthroughs. I grew up with the mentality of the early missionaries who pressed into God for their needs and for their breakthroughs. I started with a passion to push beyond my own

limitations and prove the word of God to be true. I did not sit around for someone to come by to give me a word of prophecy. I locked myself into my room and sought God until He came to speak to me. This grace has made me what I am today!

We have raised an entire generation of Charismatic and Pentecostal believers who believe it is their right to name and claim it. They believe someone is going to give them everything they need so that it will be easy in life. They use their faith to get everything they need, except to get closer to God. They press in for all the rewards of faith rather than the Author and Perfector of Faith.

The woman with the issue of blood for twelve years knew that due diligence will pay off.

> Mark 5:27-28
> *"after hearing about Jesus, she came up in the crowd behind Him and touched His cloak. For she thought, "If I just touch His garments, I will get well.""*

She heard the present word and de-programmed her twelve years of misinformation (inadequate facts) and disinformation (misleading information intended to deceive)! She then re-programmed her mind by the new truth she was receiving, breaking twelve years of old pattern and paradigm. She then charted her own course of action in her mind and implemented its reality. She took the results into her own hands.

The primary task of the pastoral ministry is to get everyone do for themselves what they should be doing for themselves. Every member has to take charge of his own progress.

> 1 Timothy 4:15
> *"Take pains with these things; be absorbed in them, so that your progress will be evident to all."*

D. Active Participation In The Church

Every member is responsible to actively participate in the life of the church. Everyone must be a participator as well as a contributor. We must not only be there in attendance but we must be positive influencers where we are. Both in the Celebration Sundays as well as in smaller groups or cell groups; the member must be a source of blessing. He must not remain on the same plane of just being a recipient of blessings but should become a giver of blessings.

Acts 20:35
""In everything I showed you that by working hard in this manner you must help the weak and remember the words of the Lord Jesus, that He Himself said, 'It is more blessed to give than to receive.'""

Every member must be trained to share in the word and not just in testimonies of what God has done for them. Every member must be taught how to minister in the gifts of prophecy and bring a word of life to those who need His counsel. Everyone must be encouraged to minister healing and deliverance to those who are oppressed by satan and sicknesses. The members must be taught to bring forth fruit and its productivity that glorifies God. So many in the churches today are consumers rather than contributors. Many are spectators rather than participators. These ignorant folks believe in the good life that others will do for them all that needs to be done and that their portion is to enjoy the benefits. They will not go to war but fight for the entitlement of the spoils of war. This Entitlement Mentality is not only destroying the political realm and national governments, but also the government of God through the church. "The government is my shepherd I shall not want ..."

The book of *Acts* carries a clear blueprint for active involvement the moment we are saved.

Acts 2:38-39
"Peter said to them, "Repent, and each of you be baptized in the name of Jesus Christ for the forgiveness of your sins; and you will receive the gift of the Holy Spirit. "For the promise is for you and

> *your children and for all who are far off, as many as the Lord our God will call to Himself.""*

"Repent, be baptised and receive the Holy Spirit. This promise of the Holy Spirit and eternal life is not only for you but also for your children's children and also for everyone connected to you even those who are a far off." (Paraphrased)

This mentality will drive the passion of the member to become useful and be a blessing to someone else. It is this mentality that will cause the members to be at their peak performance so that they can do their best for others. Then they can bring the best for those whom they are identified with.

> 1 Corinthians 14:26
> *"What is the outcome then, brethren? When you assemble, each one has a psalm, has a teaching, has a revelation, has a tongue, has an interpretation. Let all things be done for edification."*

E. Connecting In Honour To The Set Man And His Team

Every member of the House is responsible for honourably connecting to the Set Man of the House and his appointed leadership team. The ability of the member to honour the Set Man of the House will reveal the honour a person has for God's governmental authority through His delegated vessels. Most believers choose those whom they want to respect despite the fact that God has already raised men before us and has given them authority to operate in and for His Kingdom. We must choose to respect and honour those He has chosen. We respect and honour those He has blessed and is continuing to bless. We choose to honour and respect the grace and authority He has placed into their lives. In short we respect and honour what God Himself has cleansed made worthy and set apart for Himself. It is this attitude in the members that will set them apart as breakthrough believers.

Acts 11:22-23

"The news about them reached the ears of the church at Jerusalem, and they sent Barnabas off to Antioch. Then when he arrived and witnessed the grace of God, he rejoiced and began to encourage them all with resolute heart to remain true to the Lord;"

The believers who started the church in Antioch submitted the work to Barnabas because he was the sent one from the apostolic base in Jerusalem. He represented the Apostolic Team and as a sent man he carried their authority to represent them. Members must recognize the line of authority of God's government in the House. They must recognize the grace that He has given to them for His Kingdom.

Paul was not greater than Peter but each one possessed the grace to function according to what God desired. Paul knew Kingdom protocol and went to Jerusalem to submit his revelations even though he received them directly from God Himself.

Galatians 1:11-12

"For I would have you know, brethren, that the gospel which was preached by me is not according to man. For I neither received it from man, nor was I taught it, but I received it through a revelation of Jesus Christ."

Galatians 2:2

"It was because of a revelation that I went up; and I submitted to them the gospel which I preach among the Gentiles, but I did so in private to those who were of reputation, for fear that I might be running, or had run, in vain."

Galatians 2:8-9

"(for He who effectually worked for Peter in his apostleship to the circumcised effectually worked for me also to the Gentiles), and recognizing the grace that had been given to me, James and Cephas and John, who were reputed to be pillars, gave to me and Barnabas the right hand of fellowship, so that we might go to the Gentiles and they to the circumcised."

The members must honour the Set Man of the House to whom God has given His Covenant and Commission for the House. By being well related in honour of covenant, the relationship between the members and the Set Man can develop further. The process of discipleship, mentoring and fathering can then take its course. Many are reacting today to the teachings on mentoring and fathering because of their own personal fears and the abuses that immature leaders have brought about. Having taken the concerns to heart let me encourage the reader not to throw out the baby with the bath water!

The apostolic process of fathering is valid as no apostolic succession can take place without it. Even if succession has taken place the dynamics distinctive of the father will be lost in the House and in the ministry over time.

We know that the prophet Samuel carried a governmental grace that covered a geographical area of Israel.

> 1 Samuel 7:13-14
> *"So the Philistines were subdued and they did not come anymore within the border of Israel. And the hand of the LORD was against the Philistines all the days of Samuel. The cities which the Philistines had taken from Israel were restored to Israel, from Ekron even to Gath; and Israel delivered their territory from the hand of the Philistines. So there was peace between Israel and the Amorites."*

The Philistines could not come within the boundaries of Israel because Samuel's governing grace provided covering over the region. This was before the time of rulership of kings in Israel. The mantle of governmental grace was upon him to bring the nation into the obedience of faith.

> Romans 1:5
> *"through whom we have received grace and apostleship to bring about the obedience of faith among all the Gentiles for His name's sake,"*

He judged Israel for forty years and when he became older, he raised his sons to succeed him. Unfortunately, they were not able to carry the mantle of their father because they lived in sin. The governing mantle was removed from them and the whole nation was experiencing the breaking down of the hedges of protection. The Philistines had now come right within the borders of Israel and they were taking strategic positions of strength against a nation that had seen total protection from them before.

> 1 Samuel 10:5
> *""Afterward you will come to the hill of God where the Philistine garrison is; and it shall be as soon as you have come there to the city, that you will meet a group of prophets coming down from the high place with harp, tambourine, flute, and a lyre before them, and they will be prophesying."*

It was years later that David brought back the full covering of God's protection over Israel. He brought the governmental grace of Samuel's life to the next level. What he received from Samuel grew and multiplied. The governmental grace was not only able to cover Israel but it also subdued nations and kept them at peace with Israel.

> 1 Chronicles 14:17
> *"Then the fame of David went out into all the lands; and the LORD brought the fear of him on all the nations."*

The members must learn to relate accurately with the apostolic Set Man as he carries the mandate for the house. By relating in covenant and receiving his grace in impartation, the members will be able to be in proper covering and reproduce what God has deposited in the father of the House. His dreams and his legacy can continue to live on into the next generation of sons.

F. Resourcing The House Of God

Every member must learn his responsibility to resource the House of God. The members must strike a strong partnership with the House by making

available the resources they possess. Their time, talent, skills and spiritual grace must be available for the fulfilment of corporate destiny. They must surrender their possessions and financial resources to God being a faithful stewards of God's provision to the House. We are to be faithful stewards of all that has been entrusted to us for others. We must not only be custodians of the truth and revelations God has given us, but also be honourable stewards of Kingdom resources, making it available to the House for Kingdom advancement.

> 2 Corinthians 8:3-5
> *"For I testify that according to their ability, and beyond their ability, they gave of their own accord, begging us with much urging for the favor of participation in the support of the saints, and this, not as we had expected, but they first gave themselves to the Lord and to us by the will of God."*

This grace of God to show His lovingkindness through generous giving to those in need sets us apart as a distinctive kingdom community. The churches in Macedonia experienced this liberality of giving. The joy and freedom to give what we have to others who are part of our destiny and our lives are essential characteristics of true membership to the House.

Though the churches in Macedonia were experiencing difficult and trying times they rose above the ordeal of affliction by an abundance of joy with a liberality of giving. Even though they were in a state of need they begged for the privilege and favour to participate in the support of the saints.

Paul writes concerning the partnership and participation which the church at Philippi had with him:

- They participated and partnered with him for the furtherance of the gospel *(Phil 1:5)*.

- They partnered with him by sharing the grace of God on his life *(Phil 1:7)*.

- They partnered with him in friendship and companionship by seeking to do all that was pleasing to his heart. They brought joy and comfort to him *(Phil 2:1-2)*.

- They partnered with him in sufferings for the cause of Christ and the furtherance of the gospel *(Phil 1:12-14, 1:29-30)*.

- They partnered with him with their resources *(Phil 4:10-19)*.

The Philippian church's partnership was unique in that they not only laboured with him for the advancement of the Kingdom, but also for him to be blessed as a person, friend and spiritual father. Their affection for him was revealed in the sharing of their resources with him for what he desired to do for the Kingdom. They sent Epaphroditus with a large and generous gift. They wanted him to stay a while longer with Paul and minister to Paul while he was still in the confines of imprisonment. This man was sent to meet Paul's physical needs. He was Paul's companion and friend in this environment and comforted Paul by bringing the reports of the progress of the church at Philippi. However the unfavourable conditions in Rome brought about ill health and Epaphroditus came near to the point of death. But God, rich in mercy, brought about his recovery.

The church at Philippi did not send an ordinary man to minister to Paul's physical needs, but a man of stature and spiritual maturity. He was a fellow worker, a fellow soldier, a messenger and a minister to Paul's need *(Phil 2:25-30)*. He was sent to Paul to minister to him on behalf of the church at Philippi. He was representing everyone's longing and desire for Paul. Through him and through their generous giving they are confirming their deep affection and desire for meaningful partnership.

> Philippians 4:10
> *"But I rejoiced in the Lord greatly, that now at last you have revived your concern for me; indeed, you were concerned before, but you lacked opportunity."*

Paul acknowledges their commitment to resource him when all others failed to keep their consistency in the giving of their resources.

Philippians 4:15-16
"You yourselves also know, Philippians, that at the first preaching of the gospel, after I left Macedonia, no church shared with me in the matter of giving and receiving but you alone; for even in Thessalonica you sent a gift more than once for my needs."

This partnership with their resources is now placing them in the pathway of apostolic financial blessings and release.

Philippians 4:19
"And my God will supply all your needs according to His riches in glory in Christ Jesus."

Paul calls on his God to supply to all the needs of his partners who are committed and connected to him. By connecting financially and with all our other resources, our covenant relationship will take a greater depth of maturity. Every member must learn all aspects of partnership so that they can give themselves and their resources to the House they have come to identify as theirs and are part of!

G. Training For Marketplace Invasion

Every member is responsible to be trained to become an effective vessel for marketplace invasion. The church is often focused on bringing everyone into its meetings and blessing everyone with what they have prepared. This is just a small part of what God desires the church to become. God wants the church to focus on building every member so that they can be useful inside and outside of the church. We spend a maximum of about ten to twelve hours per week in church meetings. That would be a three-hour meeting, four times a week. Most ordinary believers would not reach that amount of working hours in a church. However, we spend the rest and most of our time out in the marketplace. We are involved in our families, our education, our businesses, our communities and our nation.

"All authority and power has been given back to Me both in heaven and on earth. Go therefore into all the world, preaching to them the gospel of the Kingdom and make disciples of all nations, baptising them in the Name of the Lord Jesus Christ teaching them to observe all that I have commanded you and lo I am with you always even to the end of the age." (Paraphrased – *Matt 28:18-20, Mark 16:15*)

We must train the members of our churches to move into everyone's world and influence them in their field and vocation. We must position every member in his field with a stature to influence others there and impact them with the gospel of the Kingdom.

The church has been concentrating on how to bring people into its boundaries. They desire to grow numerically. They desire to become effective organisationally and administratively. Others have done a little better by making sure all that are within the church system of operation are spiritual healthy and are devotionally accurately tuned to God and His word. This would have been sufficient if not for true apostolic emphasis and God's eternal plan. God desires to move the church out into the marketplace in order to bring God's Kingdom government into every honourable field and vocation.

> Revelations 12:10
> *"Then I heard a loud voice in heaven, saying, "Now the salvation, and the power, and the kingdom of our God and the authority of His Christ have come, for the accuser of our brethren has been thrown down, he who accuses them before our God day and night."*

The Kingdom of God will swallow up all the kingdoms of this world. It will reveal its enduring nature because it is established on righteousness, peace and joy in the Holy Ghost *(Rom 14:17)*. When everything on the earth is shaken by the word of God only that which is of God will remain. That which remains and cannot be shaken will be the Kingdom of God in demonstration.

Hebrews 12:27-29

"This expression, "Yet once more," denotes the removing of those things which can be shaken, as of created things, so that those things which cannot be shaken may remain. Therefore, since we receive a kingdom which cannot be shaken, let us show gratitude, by which we may offer to God an acceptable service with reverence and awe; for our God is a consuming fire."

Acts 16:19

"But when the master's realized that their source of income and profit was affected by Paul's ministry they seized them and dragged them into the marketplace before the authorities."

The marketplace is the last frontier to be reached as businesses, education, media, sports, medicine and politics are in this arena. The good works of integrity, honesty, wisdom, success, hard work and even professional excellence will touch and affect the lives of others around us. People are drawn to those who are winning by righteousness.

Matthew 5:16

"Let your light shine before men in such a way that they may see your good works, and glorify your Father who is in heaven."

The members must be trained within the House so that they are effective witnesses of all they have received from God each week. It must bear fruit to glorify Him.

John 15:8

""My Father is glorified by this, that you bear much fruit, and so prove to be My disciples."

The apostolic training Paul provided for the believers at Ephesus proved to be powerfully impacting, not only those within the house but all those in Asia both Jews and Greeks.

Acts 19:9-10

"But when some were becoming hardened and disobedient,

speaking evil of the Way before the people, he withdrew from them and took away the disciples, reasoning daily in the school of Tyrannus. This took place for two years, so that all who lived in Asia heard the word of the Lord, both Jews and Greeks."

The trainees were becoming so powerfully used by God that they set the precedence in the spiritual world. They took what Paul was giving them and what was Paul's (aprons and handkerchiefs) and went out everywhere healing the sick and casting out demons.

Acts 19:11-12
"God was performing extraordinary miracles by the hands of Paul, so that handkerchiefs or aprons were even carried from his body to the sick, and the diseases left them and the evil spirits went out."

Paul was not only working miracles but also raising miracle workers who were going out everywhere and affecting ordinary people in the city. They were producing such powerful results that the old dying priesthood was trying to counterfeit it. What was happening in the Apostolic base was affecting the whole city. The interaction between the Set Man and his members was creating a chain reaction and a ripple of miracles in the society. This is why every member connected to the House must be trained to become our ambassador of the Kingdom of God to influence the marketplace.

These seven vital and essential practical responsibilities must be built into every breakthrough believer. We desire to move everyone to their maximum capacity and potential until they give nothing but peak performance for the King and His Kingdom!

INTERNATIONAL STRATEGIC ALLIANCE OF APOSTOLIC CHURCHES

International Headquarters

ISAAC International Headquarters is located at Full Gospel Centre Muar, Johor, Malaysia.

The International Headquarters is the training centre for the two-week intensified "Permanent School of the Prophets" (SOP) and "God Encounter for Apostolic Reformation" (GEAR). It also provides a place for restoration, homecoming, specialized retreats, seminars and conferences.

Contact Details:
ISAAC HEADQUARTERS
c/o Wisma Mulia
No. 155, Jalan Junid Dalam, 84000 Muar, Johor,
MALAYSIA.

Tel: +606-956 1290 (O)
: +606-956 1287 (O)
Fax: +606-953 9078
E-mail Add: fgospel@streamyx.com
Website: www.jonathan-david.org

ISAAC has regional bases in more than 40 nations across the world representing five of the six inhabited continents and island groups. God is adding to that number every year. Please visit our website for more information.

TRAINING SCHOOLS BY DR. JONATHAN DAVID

Permanent School of the Prophets (SOP)

Strategies Affecting The Destiny Of Nations

- A two-week intensified training school designed to change the destiny of your life and ministry!
- To teach, train and activate individuals into the prophetic & apostolic anointing.
- To establish territorial churches for kingdom advancement.
- The establishing of the International Strategic Alliance of Apostolic Churches (ISAAC).

THE SCHOOL WITH A DYNAMIC DIFFERENCE

For more information on SOP, please visit our website:
www.jonathan-david.org

Intensive Training For ISAAC Pastors (ITIP)

To Influence The Cities and Impact the Nations

This one week intensive apostolic training is for pastors, full-time workers and those involved in the ministry who are already a covenented part of the ISAAC Network.

This training school is designed to raise apostolic and prophetic ministries that will change the spiritual landscape of their cities and nations.

For more information on ITIP, please visit our website:
www.jonathan-david.org

God Encounter for Apostolic Reformation (GEAR)

This is a unique leadership-training program designed to equip Malaysian & Singaporean pastors and leaders to minister and take their leadership to the next level.

This will be a rare opportunity to be consistently trained on the job for a full year. At each course you will get to spend two full days with God's servant, Dr. Jonathan David. You will get 8 full days of intensified training stretched over the year.

These two-day courses are a connected series of present truths that will position you to be on the cutting edge of leadership in the 21st century.

For more information on GEAR, please visit our website:
www.jonathan-david.org

Other Titles By Dr. Jonathan David

Apostolic Blueprints For Accurate Building

Many churches are built on patterns emerging from the Dark Ages, others are a recycle of the past structures to contain and maintain a past move. They have become a shadow of the past, a current reflection of what we use to have.

"Apostolic Blueprints for Accurate Building" is an overview of the original pattern anviled out through the lives and ministries of the apostles as they led the first church for kingdom advancement. This book allows us to catch a glimpse of the original church and helps us to envisage the church of the future. Perceiving these insights, will allow the apostolic builder to build to last. We can build great churches not just good churches. We can build accurately a church that will influence the city and impact the nation.

Apostolic Strategies Affecting Nations

Apostolic Strategies Affecting Nations presents proven strategies to raise up strong governing churches. These strategies provide the blueprints to raise up breakthrough believers, Senior Pastors, ministry gifts and whole churches according to the New Testament patterns. Someday all churches will be built in this manner to impact their cities and influence their nations.

"Every minister should study this book. It is truly a cutting edge present truth presentation and revelation from the heart and mind of God..."

Dr. Bill Hamon, Christian International Ministries Network, USA

"*Apostolic Strategies* is very penetrating and clearly describes the solid foundation the Church can be built on. It gives the vital insight into the next step for your church, your ministry and also for your personal life in Christ..."

Ulf Ekman, Word of Life, Uppsala, Sweden

"*Apostolic Strategies* is a book that is in the nature of the prophetic. It is a book that is 'out there in front', almost ahead of its time..."

Kevin J. Conner, Waverley Christian Fellowship, Melbourne, Australia

"The author by divine inspiration has provided the practical insight and framework for an accelerated execution of principles and purposes of the Kingdom on earth today. This masterpiece is recommended to everyone who has destiny in view..."

Dr. Tunde Bakare, The Latter Rain Assembly, Lagos, Nigeria

"There are many relevant books on the apostolic ministry but probably none as thorough and all encompassing on the subject. This is a very practical handbook for the new millennium church, yet full of insight, explanation and revelation."

Roberts Liardon, Roberts Liardon Ministry, USA

Breakthrough Thinking

A healthy renewed mind is one of the most powerful assets a believer can have in his life. Developing the mind of Christ in our thinking patterns and behaviour will release a supernatural sense of destiny of purpose and a sense of inner identity of knowing who we are in Christ.

The book provides you the keys to a proper and wholesome development of breakthrough thinking patterns that can revolutionize your behaviour and lifestyle here on this earth.

You can learn to move with the Holy Spirit in quiet confidence. You can allow divine activity to register its frequencies in your mind. You can start to allow dreams and vision of the Spirit to become an integral part of your thinking patterns. You can now live under the full inspiration of the Holy Spirit and walk in supernatural creativity of divinely inspired spontaneous thoughts. This is your time to move out of the box of religion and status quo. Explore your full capacity as an individual by walking into Breakthrough Thinking.

Decade Of Destiny

'Decade of Destiny' will empower prophetic leaders and believers to navigate through the un-chartered waters of the future. This book is immersed in prophetic revelation, giving the believer an accurate perception of the predestined future of the sons of the kingdom. This foresight into God's end-time purposes will give each nation a choice for their future, as an alternative to that which the enemy would attempt to bring about.

These revelations will keep the church from deception and false doctrine, which are sent to deceive even the elect. They will keep us on the pulse of what God is saying and doing, providing us a glimpse into the mind of the Spirit and into the heart of God for the nations.

Prayer warriors and prophetic intercessors can use God's revealed word to revoke the decrees of the enemy and place a restraining order on the activities of the devil. This book is an indispensable tool to accelerate and quicken the move of God in the hearts of the sons of the kingdom among the nations.

Catching The Waves Of Revival

This apostolic teaching is a journey towards revival. It provides insights of the different stages of revival and how we can prepare ourselves to become involved with God and His purposes at every stage of divine activity in our quest for full-scale revival and city transformation. It reveals how whole churches can be prepared to be carriers of revival flames.

This book allows the believer to chart the course of revival by discovering at what stage of revival they are in and work towards the next level. It provides strategies on how to consolidate each step of the way towards city transformation. This excellent work allows us to prepare systematically and plan strategically our corporate journey towards the full manifestation of the Holy Spirit's power on this earth for breakthroughs in the city, revival in the land and outpouring in the church.

Moving In The Gifts Of Revelation & Prophecy

The gifts of the Holy Spirit empower believers to function as effective vessels demonstrating the relevance of the Gospel today. This book lays clear apostolic foundation for the release of all the vocal and revelation gifts paving the way for the breaking forth of the power gifts.

This excellent workable strategy allows the believer to understand how to move in simple prophecy and also how to develop their giftings to the next level. This book allows the believer to progress in their prophetic anointing until the prophetic ministry can become evident in their lives.

This clear apostolic teaching allows a believer to know where they are in the prophetic anointing and helps them develop it to the next level. The comprehensive teaching provides valuable insights of how to develop the revelation gifts of the word of knowledge, the words of wisdom and the discerning of spirits. It also gives apostolic procedures and practice of how to employ them within the context of the local Church.

This book is an indispensable tool for all who want to move in prophecy and the revelation gifts. It allows you to build the base of operation for the quick and effective release of the gifts of power.

Business Sense For Making Dollars

God has given us the power to make wealth and the wisdom to administer it for kingdom advancement. This power to make wealth is released to confirm His Covenant with us. The power to make wealth, the power to gather wealth, the power to discover wealth, the power to administer wealth is released to us by the God as we are yielded to the Holy Spirit's divine activity and work in our lives. This book provides the ageless wisdom of God moving through ordinary lives to protect us from financial crisis both individually and corporately.

The first section deals solely on the Asian regional crisis. How the Asian economic bubble burst, and how the contingent effect spread and why. The second section deals with the corporate business crisis and the apostolic strategy for its recovery. How each corporate business can remove the constrains of business and implement growth strategies for breakthrough in financial abundance. The last section deals with the personal financial crisis and the steps each one of us can take for personal financial breakthrough. God has given a ministry to the wicked; "a task of gathering and collecting so that he may give it to one who is good in God's sight" (*Eccl. 2:26*). How do we prepare for the end-time wealth transfer?

Other resources by Dr. Jonathan David are also available such as: Teaching CDs and Teaching DVDs.

For the full range of resources by Dr. Jonathan David, please visit our website: **www.jonathan-david.org**